Andes 2020:
A New Strategy for the Challenges of Colombia and the Region

Report of an Independent Commission
Sponsored by the Council on Foreign Relations
Center for Preventive Action

Daniel W. Christman and
John G. Heimann, Co-Chairs
Julia E. Sweig, Project Director

Founded in 1921, the Council on Foreign Relations is an independent, national member-ship organization and a nonpartisan center for scholars dedicated to producing and dis-seminating ideas so that individual and corporate members, as well as policymakers, journalists, students, and interested citizens in the United States and other countries, can better understand the world and the foreign policy choices facing the United States and other governments. The Council does this by convening meetings; conducting a wide-ranging Studies program; publishing *Foreign Affairs*, the preeminent journal covering inter-national affairs and U.S. foreign policy; maintaining a diverse membership; sponsoring Inde-pendent Task Forces; and providing up-to-date information about the world and U.S. foreign policy on the Council's website, www.cfr.org.

THE COUNCIL TAKES NO INSTITUTIONAL POSITION ON POLICY ISSUES AND HAS NO AFFILIATION WITH THE U.S. GOVERNMENT. STATEMENTS OF FACT AND EXPRESSIONS OF OPINION CONTAINED IN ITS PUBLICA-TIONS ARE THE SOLE RESPONSIBILITY OF THE AUTHOR OR AUTHORS.

The Council will sponsor an Independent Commission when (1) an issue of current and critical importance to U.S. foreign policy arises, and (2) it seems that a group diverse in backgrounds and perspectives may, nonetheless, be able to reach a meaningful consensus on a policy through private and nonpartisan deliberations. Typically, a Commission meets between two and five times over a brief period to ensure the relevance of its work.

Upon reaching a conclusion, a Commission issues a report, and the Council publishes its text and posts it on the Council website. Commission reports can take three forms: (1) a strong and meaningful policy consensus, with Commission members endorsing the general policy thrust and judgments reached by the group, though not necessarily every finding and recommendation; (2) a report stating the various policy positions, each as sharply and fairly as possible; or (3) a "Chairman's Report," where Commission members who agree with the chairman's report may associate themselves with it, while those who disagree may submit dissenting statements. Upon reaching a conclusion, a Commission may also ask indi-viduals who were not members of the Commission to associate themselves with the Com-mission report to enhance its impact. All Commission reports "benchmark" their findings against current administration policy in order to make explicit areas of agreement and disagreement. The Commission is solely responsible for its report. The Council takes no institutional position.

For further information about the Council or this Commission report, please write to the Council on Foreign Relations, 58 East 68th Street, New York, NY 10021, or call the Director of Communications at 212-434-9400. Visit our website at www.cfr.org.

CONTENTS

FOREWORD

Over the past two decades, the White House and Congress have dedicated substantial resources to promote order and stability in Colombia and the greater Andean region. Yet even with this considerable help from the U.S. government, the region continues to suffer—from political instability, economic stagnancy, widening inequality, and decreasing physical security due to ongoing violent conflict and porous borders that enable the easy movement of drugs and arms. Regional collapse is a possibility, something that would constitute a major setback, not simply for U.S. interests in the hemisphere but also for the world.

The Council, in conjunction with Inter-American Dialogue, first focused on the Andean region during the debate in 1999 over Plan Colombia, through the creation of an Independent Task Force on Colombia. At the same time, the Council's National Program convened an adjunct Task Force in California. The two Task Forces published reports with substantially different views. The first endorsed the general thrust of Plan Colombia, whereas the second, taking a skeptical view of the merits of pursuing a drug war, emphasized the need for broader economic and social programs.

In 2002, two years after Congress voted for Plan Colombia, the Council's Latin America Program and the Center for Preventive Action joined forces to once again examine the regional dimensions of the Colombia conflict and the effect of U.S. policy in the Andes. This report of the Council on Foreign Relations's Center for Preventive Action offers a full range of recommendations for the United States, the international community, and the Andean nations themselves to prevent collapse and set the region on a path to democracy, prosperity, and security. The result is *Andes 2020: A New Strategy for the Challenges of Colombia and the Region.*

Andes 2020 highlights the critical need for regional solutions to problems that are increasingly regional in nature. It also highlights the importance of land reform and rural development. The report calls on Congress and the Bush administration to reorient U.S. and international engagement, including adopting a shared strategy to reduce demand for drugs in consuming countries.

Preventive Action Commission Chairmen Daniel W. Christman and John G. Heimann, distinguished leaders in their respective fields of security and finance, led a group of over twenty scholars, practitioners, and regional policy experts. The Commission also benefited from the dedication and expertise of its project director, Julia E. Sweig, and the director of the Center for Preventive Action, William L. Nash. My deepest appreciation goes to each of them for helping to produce this important piece of work.

I also want to express my thanks to the Hewlett Foundation and the Ford Foundation. Financial support from these two organizations, to the Center for Preventive Action and the Latin America Program respectively, has been critical to this initiative.

It is my hope that the vision for a new American and international strategy set forth in this report will reinvigorate the public debate and lead to a more comprehensive and effective policy toward a region that is critical to U.S. interests.

Richard N. Haass
President
Council on Foreign Relations
January 2004

ACKNOWLEDGMENTS

This project thrived with the help of many—and the inspiration of a few—critical individuals. The first is Leslie H. Gelb, president emeritus of the Council on Foreign Relations. Well before Andes 2020 was even a thought, Les gave me the necessary resources to think hard about Colombia and the Andes, the confidence not to fear bucking the conventional wisdom, and his inimitable gift of high expectations.

When William L. Nash banged on my door one summer day in 2002 to ask if I would consider working on a Center for Preventive Action (CPA) initiative on the Andes, my first thought was to politely decline and return to the peace and quiet of my own thoughts and writing. But Bill's intellectual honesty, enthusiasm, and camaraderie are hard to resist, and I soon came to reassess the chance to work with him as an opportunity I could not turn down. I am grateful for Bill's collegiality, trust, and friendship.

One of the Council's greatest assets is the opportunity it presents senior fellows to learn from the best Americans working on the global stage. Before establishing Andes 2020, I had not met the two individuals who became our co-chairs, Daniel W. Christman and John G. Heimann. Their wisdom, patience, intelligence, and sheer endurance are an inspiration to all of us who have worked on this project. I am grateful to each of them separately, and to both of them together, for their skillful co-chairmanship of this very diverse Commission, their constant encouragement to the project staff, and their genuine commitment to adding a serious voice to the Latin America policy debate.

Michael Marx McCarthy, my research associate, and Kathleen M. Jennings, Bill Nash's research associate, tirelessly and intelligently coordinated every aspect of this project, from the sublime to the ridiculous. They each made significant contributions in the realm of ideas and research and drafted substantial portions of the report—all while juggling administrative, travel, and other related logistical details. Both highly competent young professionals with exciting careers ahead of them, they represent the best the Council has to offer.

A number of colleagues at the Council provided support and guidance of one sort or another. My thanks go to Kenneth Maxwell, director of the Latin America Program, who recognized the importance of teaming up with Bill Nash and the Center for Preventive Action and readily embraced the project. Thanks also go to Council President Richard Haass, Michael Peters, Lawrence Korb, James Lindsay, Robert Orr, Lee Feinstein, Janice Murray, Patricia Dorff, Lisa Shields, Irina Faskianos, Anne Luzzatto, Rossana Ivanova, Abigail Zoba, and Janine Hill.

Cristina Eguizabal of the Ford Foundation has been a forceful support to me and to the Council's Latin America Program. She has my thanks.

Alexander Sarly worked as a research consultant at the Council for most of the lifespan of this project. He researched and designed the graphical data in Appendix B. Jeremy Weinstein, now at the Center for Global Development, contributed a great deal with ideas and drafts. My heartfelt thanks go to each of them.

Our trips to Colombia, Venezuela, and Ecuador were most enriching, serving as the core of our extensive consultation process and providing a crucial complement to the dozens more visits held in Washington and New York. Commission observer Ed Jardine, who is based in Caracas, went beyond the call of duty in arranging a number of meetings and activities for the group during our visit to Venezuela. The same is true of Gustavo Marturet. Each has my thanks. Likewise, Kelly McBride provided invaluable assistance on the ground in Bogotá. A list of those we met in the region and in the United States appears in Appendix E. On behalf of the Commission's co-chairs, members, and staff, I extend thanks to all those who took the time to meet with us. I am also grateful to the U.S. ambassadors whom we met: Ambassador Anne Patterson, then in Colombia; Ambassador Charles Shapiro in Venezuela; and Ambassador Kristie A. Kenney in Ecuador. Our exchanges with them and their teams were most informative. In turn, I am grateful to the ambassadors in Washington representing Colombia,

Venezuela, and Ecuador. The assistance they provided was critical to the success of our visits to their countries.

Finally, I want to thank all the members of the Andes 2020 Commission. They approached this process with a spirit of openness and civility, an increasingly precious commodity in today's foreign policy debates but one always present at the Council. They made substantial contributions to the substance and argument of the report and were exceedingly generous with their time. It was a pleasure to work with them.

Julia E. Sweig
Project Director

THE ANDEAN REGION

Source: Alternative Development and Eradication: A Failed Balance, Transnational Institute Briefing Series, March 2002, No. 4, available at www.tni.org.

EXECUTIVE SUMMARY

The democracies of the Andean region—Colombia, Venezuela, Ecuador, Peru, and Bolivia—are at risk. The problems that characterize other developing regions—including political instability, economic stagnancy, widening inequality, and social divisions along class, color, ethnic, ideological, and urban-rural fault lines—are all present in the Andes. Most important is the region's physical insecurity, due in some countries to ongoing or resurgent violent conflict, and in every country to the lack of state control over significant territory and to porous borders that enable the easy movement of drugs, arms, and conflict. Equally sobering, expectations for strong democracy and economic prosperity in the Andes remain unrealized. Recognizing its interests, the United States over the past two decades has invested billions of dollars and significant manpower to stem the flow of illegal drugs from the region northward; to assist local security forces in the fight against drugs, terror, and insurgency; and to promote free markets, human rights, and democratic consolidation. Yet the region remains on the brink of collapse, an outcome that would pose a serious threat to the U.S. goal of achieving democracy, prosperity, and security in the hemisphere.

The United States has attempted to counter the region's vulnerability through Plan Colombia and the Andean Counterdrug Initiative (ACI). Plan Colombia was crafted in 1999 and will end in 2005, whereas the ACI is an annual appropriation. Many dedicated public servants and private citizens in the United States and the Andes have worked together to strengthen democracy and security in the region. Rather than suggesting a strategy to steadily reduce the commitment of the United States to Colombia and the Andean region, this Commission outlines what it favors as the next stage of U.S. engagement after Plan Colombia concludes, with an eye toward preventing the outbreak of major conflict and mitigating current levels of violence.

The security crisis in the Andes is the most significant in the Western Hemisphere, one that exacts a direct toll on American lives and interests. However, in the broader context of U.S. foreign policy—and despite the ample bipartisan support that exists to sustain the current commitment of approximately $700 million per year to the region—the Commission recognizes that an increase in U.S. government dollars for Colombia and the Andes is unlikely. In fact, more money may not be the solution to the region's problems. The Commission's principal proposal is a reallocation of the U.S. financial and political commitment to reflect the strategic objectives in this report. The Commission recognizes that, within both Congress and the executive branch, a good deal of discussion is underway on how to prepare for Plan Colombia's end. It is the Commission's hope that this report will contribute to that debate by setting forth possible directions for continued engagement that delivers improved and sustainable results for local governments and the region's citizens, as well as serving U.S. interests in the Andes.

The strategy outlined in this report is built on the widely shared belief that sustainable, peaceful democracies in the Andean region depend as much on political, legal, and socioeconomic reform—including the implementation of wide-ranging development initiatives targeted to the poor majorities and disenfranchised rural populations—as on "hard" counternarcotics and counterterror initiatives. *Andes 2020* thus addresses what the Commission considers to be a major weakness of current U.S. policy, as embodied in Plan Colombia and the ACI: too great an emphasis on counternarcotics and security issues, and too little emphasis on complementary, comprehensive, regional strategies.

The Commission's work is shaped by three imperatives designed to rectify the limitations of current policy. First is the need to diffuse and more equitably distribute political and economic resources and power in each country. Second is the importance of greater participation from the broader international community across the range of diplomatic, political, economic, social, security, and humanitarian issues in the region. Third is the recognition that regional problems with regional impact require regional approaches, and that greater cooperation among the Andean countries is essential to successfully tackle shared challenges. To that end, U.S. policy can be more effectively organized to recognize the regional dimension of the Andean crisis, rather than sticking to a strictly bilateral, country-by-country approach.

The Commission believes that the security environment in Colombia and the Andes is sufficiently vulnerable to merit continued U.S. support for counterdrug and counterterrorism programs. Rather than being one critical element of a broader policy agenda, however, these programs now receive the vast majority of U.S. resources for the region. That imbalance will have to change over time, with some of the money now spent to combat "drugs and thugs" devoted instead to new priorities. These include sustainable rural and border development, including strategic land reform; political reforms to strengthen the rule of law and consolidate democratic institutions through increased accountability and transparency; trade and economic development, including increased access to markets and legitimate economic opportunities; and a multilateral counterdrug policy that also addresses the issue of demand in consuming countries. This report argues that determined action on these three strategic objectives will, over time, accomplish sustainable progress on political, economic, and security goals that a policy focused mainly on supply-side counterdrug efforts cannot achieve.

Within the Andes, Colombia is the linchpin. The severity of Colombia's internal conflict—combined with its size, importance in the narcotics trade, economic influence, and the borders it shares with three of the four other Andean states—means that success in moving the country toward peace could shore up democracy and security in the entire region. Failure could have the opposite effect. Venezuela and Ecuador are particularly vulnerable to spillover from Colombia's conflict—narcotraffickers and the three Colombian illegal armed groups already use the vast border regions for operations—placing those neighbors most at risk should Colombia's conflict further weaken the Colombian state. Accordingly, this report focuses primarily on Colombia, Venezuela, and Ecuador, though, given the regional dimension and scope of the challenges facing the Andes, many of the proposed policy recommendations are directly relevant to Bolivia and Peru.

Andes 2020 is organized into four sections, followed by appendixes containing additional technical recommendations, statistics, and graphs. The first section, Findings, describes the extent of the crisis in the Andes, analyzes past and present U.S. policy toward the region, outlines the core of a new U.S. strategy—including the importance of improved interagency policy coordination at senior levels—and identifies three key strategic objectives for improving governance and security in the region. The first objective is major investment of financial and political resources in rural areas, with a commitment to strategic rural land reform. The second is increased engagement by the entire international community across the range of diplomatic, political, economic, and humanitarian issues at play in the region. Third is the development, both within the Andes and by the United States and the international community, of regional approaches to regional problems.

In the second section, Land Reform and Rural Development, the Commission advocates comprehensive policies for the political and economic development and integration of the rural Andes. Recommendations for the Andean governments include the imposition and enforcement of property taxes; the acceleration of land titling and registry; and the enactment of strategic, market-assisted land reform in an accountable and transparent fashion. On the latter point, the Commission strongly recommends that the Colombian government—with U.S. assistance—halt the ongoing coercive land grab by left-wing guerrillas, right-wing paramilitaries, and narcotraffickers. It is also crucial that Colombia's asset forfeiture laws are effectively applied to ill-gotten land gains now in the hands of Colombia's illegal armed actors and drug traffickers.

The third section, U.S. and International Community Engagement, lays out strategies for effective multilateral engagement in the region, particularly in the fight against illegal drugs and on economic and humanitarian issues. Regarding illegal drugs, the Commission recommends a multilateral, multifaceted approach that combines financial incentives, broad international participation, and shared responsibility on both the supply and demand sides of the problem. This can be achieved through the establishment of a special development fund for drug-cultivating countries, administered by the World Bank and sponsored by the major drug-consuming countries. Other recommendations include a coordinated regional assistance strategy by international donors; targeted financial sanctions against narcotraffickers, paramilitaries, guerrillas, and their financial supporters; and greater human and financial resources to stem Colombia's humanitarian crisis. Recognizing the primacy of the U.S. role in promoting human rights and providing security assistance to Colombia and the region, the Commission also proposes actions to improve U.S. security assistance. Foremost among these is raising the current cap on the number of U.S. military and contract personnel permitted to conduct training of Colombian armed forces, thereby accelerating their professionalization. In a similar vein, the Commission recommends revising the current fixed ratio of military-to-civilian personnel, in order to offer the commander of the U.S. Southern Command (South Com) greater flexibility and discretion in directing the use of military and contract resources. These changes cannot compromise the U.S. commitment to upholding human rights in its security assistance programs.

The fourth section, Regional Approaches to Regional Problems, contains strategies to leverage regional capabilities and strengths in pursuit of collective and national interests in the areas of security, trade, economic development, anticorruption efforts, and humanitarian action. On issues where common problems exist but a cross-border approach is not viable, the Commission's recommendations focus on actions that can be taken by individual states but that are, in principle, applicable to all Andean countries. One such common recommendation is the need to strengthen the revenue-generating systems of the Andes by cracking down on tax evasion, broadening the tax base, and moving toward a more progressive tax structure. The Commission also recommends that the Andean governments work together to negotiate an Andean Free Trade Agreement (AFTA) until the advent of the Free Trade Area of the Americas (FTAA); form an Andean customs union with reduced intraregional tariff barriers; take greater action against the humanitarian crisis spilling over Colombia's borders; and expand security cooperation between armed forces along border areas.

In sum, the problems in the Andes are acute but not unmanageable. The United States's longstanding commitment to the region can show major progress only with senior U.S. leadership and a reallocation of resources, with a particular emphasis on rural initiatives, political and socioeconomic reform, and a multilateral approach to drug control—on both the supply and demand sides.

FINDINGS

A POTENTIALLY FAILING REGION

The Andean region of Latin America—defined by the Andes mountain chain and including Venezuela, Colombia, Ecuador, Peru, and Bolivia—is in peril. In the last two decades, per capita economic growth has been close to zero, meaning that the average adult in these five nations has seen no improvement in his or her income over his or her lifetime. In particular, rural populations live in a state of extreme risk, often facing threats to their physical security and almost uniformly enduring a lack of effective services and legitimate economic opportunity.

Democracy in the Andean region—home to more than 120 million people—is threatened by staggering inequality and poverty, weak political institutions, habitual impunity for human rights violations, corruption, marginal regard for the rule of law, and lack of state control over parts of its territory. Common characteristics of most or all Andean states include the concentration of political and economic power; exclusion of rural populations; violent conflict; and transnational security threats fueled by drugs, other illegal industries, criminals, illegal armed groups, and narcotraffickers.

The U.S. Agency for International Development (USAID) defines failing states as "countries in which the government is steadily losing the ability to perform its basic functions of governance and is losing legitimacy ... with varying conditions that may lead to civil and communal strife or that may have resulted from such conflict; humanitarian crises, such as starvation and mass refugee movements; and increasing criminality and widespread corruption." By this definition, each nation in the Andean region is, to varying degrees, either failing or potentially failing. Moreover, because of the similarities of each nation's economic, governance, and security problems (which are especially prevalent in the rural areas adjoining border regions), and the region's inchoate collective security capacity, illegal armed groups, narcotraffickers, and other criminal syndicates have ample scope for operations—thus further exacerbating domestic and regional vulnerabilities and raising the specter of a failing Andean region.[1]

Given its location, economic influence, population, political system, illicit industries, and internal conflict, Colombia is the linchpin. Success or failure in moving the country toward peace will have consequences for democracy and security in the entire region, most severely for Venezuela and Ecuador, its neighbors to the east and south, respectively. Because these countries' border regions are frequently utilized by narcotraffickers and by Colombia's three illegal armed actors—the Revolutionary Armed Forces of Colombia (FARC), the National Liberation Army (ELN), and the United Self-Defense Forces of Colombia (AUC)—to carry out activities, Ecuador and Venezuela are the nations most immediately vulnerable to Colombia's conflict.[2] Therefore, because in the Commission's

---

[1]The Andean states of Colombia, Venezuela, Ecuador, Peru, and Bolivia are formally linked by geography (the Andes mountain chain) and membership in the Andean Community Secretariat, but each has a complex, specific history. In fact, even through the 1990s, their dissimilar experiences with democratic rule complicated efforts to amalgamate the nations of the Andes into a unit for analysis. Ecuador, Peru, and Bolivia gradually democratized in the 1990s, after habitual interruptions of democratic order during the 1970s and 1980s. Over the same period, Colombia and Venezuela's stable democracies slowly unwound. However, as the drug trade broadened across borders and Colombia's conflict intensified and regionalized in impact, a convergence of threats emerged across the Andes. As this report notes, U.S. policy sought to address the region's challenges primarily through supply-side counterdrug efforts, a trade preferences regime for the Andes (minus Venezuela), military assistance with human rights standards, and a focus on Colombia. This policy helped awaken some nations to the regional nature of security threats, to which the Andean Community Secretariat has responded with joint declarations on security and drug interdiction and policies to increase trade integration and inaugurate a region-wide customs union. Concrete cooperation, however, still suffers from the historical inability of Andean nations to move beyond paralyzing domestic political and economic crises and focus on a mutually beneficial foreign policy, a trend that the region has only recently begun to reverse.

[2]The FARC, ELN, and AUC are each listed on the U.S. State Department's list of foreign terrorist organizations, and U.S. and Colombian officials regularly call them "narcoterrorists." In the narrative of this report, the Commission describes them as "illegal armed groups," a phrase that accurately describes their status as rebels. The groups are commonly referred to in the press as insurgencies (FARC, ELN) and paramilitary forces (AUC), and the Commission takes into account the respective implications of these distinct categories in its findings and recommendations. See Appendix C for the State Department's assessment of these groups in its *Patterns of Global Terrorism* for 2003.

view Colombia is most critical to overall regional stability and security, and Venezuela and Ecuador are most affected by that nation's progress or slide, the focus of this report is on those three Andean nations.[3]

U.S. policy in the Andes has reached a tipping point. Over the last twenty years, the United States has spent more than $25 billion in the Andes, primarily on a drug war focused on supply-side eradication and interdiction—an effort that has not been accompanied by an equivalent focus on development, institution building, and necessary public- and private-sector reforms in the region, nor by a comprehensive, multilateral demand-reduction strategy in drug-consuming nations.[4] An aggressive, comprehensive regional strategy from the United States, the international community, and local actors is urgently needed: a strategy that goes beyond drugs to channel resources to far-reaching rural and border development and judicial and security reform, and that will mobilize the commitment and capital of local elites, as well as U.S. and other international resources. Without such a strategy, the collapse of Andean governments is far more likely, and the simmering conflict in the region could escalate beyond a regional security and humanitarian crisis to directly threaten the stability of the Western Hemisphere. In this troubling scenario, the United States would face a fundamentally different array of policy options, the most aggressive of which could require a military commitment beyond what

---

[3]The collapse of the Gonzalo Sanchez de Lozada government in Bolivia in October 2003, and the repercussions (including increased skepticism toward U.S. policy) felt around the region—most prominently in Peru and Ecuador, with their sizeable indigenous populations—sent a serious message to U.S. and Andean leaders. Bolivia's collapse could be a harbinger of a broader regional disintegration if an objective assessment of policy failures is not undertaken. More ominously, if the current volatility in Colombia or Venezuela boils over to a collapse of either sitting government, the consequences will be immeasurably more devastating to regional stability and U.S. standing in Latin America.

[4]Drug Policy Alliance, www.drugpolicy.org/global/drugpolicyby/latinamerica/; Peter Reuter, *The Limits of Supply-Side Drug Control*, RAND Institute, 2001; Russell Crandall, *Driven by Drugs*, Lynne Rienner Publishers, 2002, pp. 30–35. Since 2000 alone, the United States has provided over $2 billion to Colombia and over $1 billion to the rest of the Andes, mostly skewed toward counterdrug and security assistance.

the U.S. Congress and public would support. To head off this destructive course, it is time for the U.S. government to undertake a qualitative policy shift toward a cohesive and holistic strategy to mitigate conflict and prevent state failure in the Andes.

The Mandate of Andes 2020 and the Future of Bolivia and Peru

Although the work of this Commission is focused on Colombia, Venezuela, and Ecuador, Peru and Bolivia are also critical to Andean stability. However, in comparison to Ecuador and Venezuela, Peru and Bolivia have ancillary relationships with Colombia. Thus, because the Commission correlates the success or failure of the region with the likelihood of success in Colombia, Peru and Bolivia represent less severe threats. Given the regional dimension and scope of problems identified in this report, however, many of the proposed policy recommendations are directly relevant to those two countries.

Although the resignation of President Gonzalo Sanchez de Lozada in October 2003 ended the political violence stemming from ongoing strife in Bolivia, the Commission recognizes that the current peace may be temporary and that the prospect of explosive conflict cannot be ruled out. In particular, the Commission is concerned about the negative consequences for democracy in Bolivia and the Andes if an extra-constitutional change of government occurs. Bolivia, the poorest nation in South America, is nearing insolvency; it suffers from acute ethnic and racial conflict over coca, land, water, gas, and the distribution of other state services; and the political consensus that once held the country together has collapsed. In the 1990s, Bolivia was considered by the United States and the international financial institutions (IFIs) as a model for reform in the Andes, taking the right steps to fight the drug war and liberalize the economy. Today, almost everything is going wrong in the country and Bolivians regard the U.S. government and its policies with great skepticism.

In Peru, meanwhile, recovery from two decades of internal conflict and authoritarian rule is fragile. Although economic growth has occurred, political instability remains. Insufficient state presence, grinding poverty, and persistent political crises all conspire to make Peru's highlands increasingly vulnerable to the reemergence of illegal actors and repressive forces of its past. The recent findings of a government-appointed Truth and Reconciliation Commission have further shaken Peruvian society. That Commission found that more than 69,000 Peruvians, mostly Quechua-speaking Indians, were killed between 1980 and 2000, primarily by the virulent Shining Path insurgency but also by state security and citizen militia forces.

Therefore, in light of Bolivia's profound crisis and Peru's tenuous democratic renewal, this Commission recommends that the Center for Preventive Action devote a follow-up report entirely to Peru and Bolivia.

STAGNANT ECONOMIES, FRAGILE DEMOCRATIC INSTITUTIONS, AND WEAK RULE OF LAW

Growth in the Andean region's legitimate economies ranges from anemic and inconsistent (Colombia, Peru, and Ecuador) to stagnant or contracting (Venezuela and Bolivia).[5] Although the Andean economies have avoided major meltdowns in the last couple of years, none is strong enough to withstand a global economic crisis. Indeed, government budgets are heavily burdened by domestic and foreign debt payments. And as international capital markets are essentially dried up for the region, past promises that trade integration, macroeconomic reforms, and sound fiscal and monetary policies would bring foreign investment, growth, and prosperity are increasingly met by voter skepticism. As a result, Andean

---

[5]Although the Andean region's combined annual gross domestic product (GDP) is small relative to the United States's—$260 billion compared to $10.4 trillion—the region is an important U.S. market. In 2002, imports from the United States exceeded $11 billion, exports to the United States totaled $25 billion, and private foreign direct investment accounted for $8.7 billion, with an additional $4.2 billion in portfolio investment capital.

governments favorably disposed to joining the global economy now find that the case for liberalization is losing domestic political traction.

For a variety of reasons, the economic reforms of the 1990s did not achieve the ambitious goals that policymakers hoped would be met by now. The so-called Washington consensus did not directly hurt the poor, but nor did its reform prescriptions translate into economic gain for the poor or middle class. Indeed, the vast majority of the region's poor—ranging from 60 to 80 percent of the population—still does not have sufficient market access. For millions in the Andes, this means exclusion both from the global economy and from legitimate economic opportunities. Instead, the primary beneficiaries of the reforms were the rich.[6]

The fiscal and trade reforms of the 1990s may be inadequate because the institutional maturity necessary for economic development remains unrealized in the Andes. A fundamental problem facing the region's governments is that the nuts and bolts of functioning market economies—including credit for individual small and medium-sized enterprises; microfinance for the poor and working poor; access to property title and registry; functioning infrastructure; market-based, locally developed land reform; and progressive, equitable tax reform and enforcement—are, for the most part, absent. The reforms may also not have been implemented to the fullest extent possible.

Reasons for its shortcomings aside, it remains that the Washington consensus is not having an ameliorative impact on the Andean region at the moment. A serious reassessment—factoring in both domestic political realities and ongoing structural problems—is therefore in order. Priorities of a new economic reform strategy must include economic development initiatives for the poor majority; stimulus measures to generate growth; and actions

---

[6]Peru provides a striking example of this problem, despite experiencing 5 percent growth in 2002. Nancy Birdsall and Augusto de la Torre, *Washington Contentious: Economic Policies for Social Equity in Latin America*, Carnegie Endowment for International Peace and the Inter-American Dialogue, 2001.

to address the structural problem of income inequality, which has a negative effect on growth and poverty reduction.[7]

The lack of responsive democratic institutions—in particular, meaningful access to a functioning legal system by those other than the country's elites—complicates attempts at substantive economic and political reform. Across the region, institutional, political, and societal commitments to the rule of law remain elusive. Limited access and outright corruption mean that individual countries' judiciaries are seen as neither independent nor trustworthy. The distortive influence of oil and other extractive industries on governance, transparency, and management of revenues also undermines public confidence in the political and legal systems and the private sector. Overall, low regard for public and private institutions reinforces the countries' vulnerability to the drug industry, to populism of the left or right, and to deepening social instability.[8]

In particular, the lack of effective law enforcement and prosecutorial power—combined with weak social welfare systems—enables the drug trade and black market industries, and those who directly and indirectly benefit from them, to thrive in the Andes. This allows the cultivation and processing of coca and opium to flourish in Colombia and return to Peru and Bolivia; easy transit through, and supply of precursor chemicals and weapons from, Ecuador and Venezuela; and access to illegal markets and money-laundering facilities in Brazil, Colombia, the United States, and Europe. This problem affects the United States directly: the Andean region supplies the illicit U.S. drug market with approximately 80 percent of its cocaine and over 50 percent of its heroin.[9]

---

[7]A recent World Bank study determined that income inequality in the region widened over the past thirty years, with the effect of slowing poverty reduction and directly hindering growth. *Inequality in Latin America: Breaking with History?* The World Bank, March 7, 2003.

[8]See Appendix B for graphs on poverty, inequality, concentration of land and wealth, and tax revenue.

[9]Although Colombia is not responsible for a significant portion of the world's poppy cultivation (the crop used to make heroin), heroin originating from that country represents a majority of the supply in the United States. See *International Narcotics Control Strategy Report—2002*, U.S. Department of State Bureau for International Narcotics and Law Enforcement Affairs, 2003, www.state.gov/g/inl/rls/nrcrpt/2002/.

THE CRITICAL ROLE OF ELITES

The Commission regards elites in the Andean region as critical to the success or failure of the conflict prevention strategies recommended in this report. We recognize that the nature and relative power of elites—whether political, economic, or both—is different and fluid in each of the countries considered. As a whole, however, elites in the Andes typically wield power through informal means such as political machines, powerful family firms, or the corruption of authorities. These informal instruments may make elites in these societies more powerful than in countries with stronger formal institutions that are more able to resist co-optation or personalization. Accordingly, elites often resist the strengthening of formal institutions, because this would attenuate their power.

By "elites," the Commission refers to holders of strategic positions in powerful political or economic organizations and movements who are able to affect political outcomes regularly and significantly. This definition includes those in the upper financial and business strata as well as political elites, such as politicians and powerful labor and trade union leaders. Elites are able to maintain their power because they are in a position to either withstand or undermine—or support and strengthen—the countervailing institutional pressures of democratic rule, such as an independent judiciary, a free press, and state agencies that collect taxes, enforce the law, generate accountability, and provide other basic services to the population.

Yet the nature of elites, especially political elites, is changing in Latin America. Nonestablishment figures now occupy important posts in the legislatures, foreign ministries, mayoral and local councils, and executive branches across the region. There are also "dissident" elites—representing a distinct faction of the traditional leadership base—and "new" elites, consisting of an emerging generation of powerful citizens not linked to a traditional power group. In most cases, these two sets of elites counterbalance existing power structures by working for reform measures that are genuinely focused on the common good of their country. However, these dissident and new elites face many barriers to achieving their goals, primarily due to the nexus of weak democratic institutions and traditional elite groups' control of political and economic levers of power.

The Commission believes that there is room for constructive U.S. policy engagement with Andean elites, whether dissident, new, or traditional. Specifically, Washington, other interested governments, and the multilateral development community can encourage and pressure elites into playing a more constructive role in their countries by, for example, bolstering good governance and anticorruption initiatives through nongovernmental channels, and directly supporting democratic institution building by paying income and property taxes and adhering to the rule of law. A strategy of constructive U.S. and international engagement with local elites would leverage the common interests of both sides in strengthening democratic governance and security in the region—crucial elements in attracting foreign and domestic investment and achieving economic growth.

PAST AND CURRENT U.S. POLICY: NOT NEGLECT—MYOPIA

In crafting a new strategy for the region, it is first important to understand the direction of past and current U.S. policy. Although the United States is criticized for inattention to the region, the Commission considers myopia, not neglect, to be the principal problem. Andean issues related to the drug war, trade integration, liberalization and macroeconomic reform, financial solvency, Colombia's security crisis, human rights, and democracy promotion have occupied important, although intermittent, senior-level U.S. attention in the last two decades. The considerable time, energy, and political commitment dedicated to these initiatives delivered significant results. As currently practiced, however, the limited scope of the agenda underestimates the fundamental challenges to the region, undermining the efficacy of current U.S. policy and preventing structural problems from being addressed.

Both the United States and leaders of the political classes in the Andes bear significant responsibility for the region's growing risk of fiscal, political, and security collapse.[10] First, U.S. policy has dedicated a disproportionate amount of financial, institutional, and diplomatic capital to the drug war, failing to integrate resources spent in this area with other essential elements of reform. In particular, as U.S. policymakers focused their energies and funds into counternarcotics programs, they did not simultaneously work to build multilateral support for the sustained investment and engagement needed to strengthen the region's legitimate economies. Nor has there been an ongoing, collective approach to the demand side of the drug problem in consuming countries. The narrow scope of U.S. policy is exacerbated by the attitude of many Andean elites. As already noted, elites in the region have long preferred to conduct business outside of formal institutions bound by the rule of law. Institutions capable of collecting revenue, enforcing the law, resolving judicial disputes, building roads and bridges, distributing water and electricity, and other fundamentals of a functioning market economy and a modern, democratic nation have therefore received grossly inadequate support from the classes of people best situated to construct them.

These two phenomena—disproportionate attention to the supply side of the drug war by the United States and neglect of democratic institutions and the expansion of market access by the elite—reinforce each other. And although inattention itself is not the direct cause of the problems, it will take senior-level U.S. attention to break this cycle and to seriously engage the regions' elites in the process.

Thus, without a new U.S. strategy that addresses the structural vulnerabilities within and across borders in the region—and the commitment of local elites to pay taxes in order to finance the legitimate state institutions that make countries function—U.S. tax dollars spent on spraying illicit crops, protecting oil pipelines, and prosecuting a counterinsurgency war will be wasted. Ensuring the

---

[10]The Commission notes that the myriad problems present in Colombia and the Andes have been largely neglected—in terms of resource commitments—by important members of the European Union and the international community.

success of future reform programs will require a concerted effort by Washington to work with regional leaders to substantially overhaul and recreate domestic institutions, and to build alliances with multilateral institutions and other bilateral donors committed to sustainable strategies for long-term development in the region.

THE CORE OF A NEW U.S. STRATEGY

The United States is the agenda-setter for regional policy and the major market for everything the region produces, legal or otherwise. However, the region's slide in recent years has occurred as U.S. policies in the Andes—prioritized roughly in the order of counternarcotics, counterterrorism, opening markets to free trade, and promoting democracy—have remained relatively fixed, with minimal revision to reflect the threats posed by the region's deepening crisis. Considering the faith U.S. policymakers placed in these policies, the inability of the United States to assess the changing conditions in the Andes and reorient its policies to deal with the deteriorating situation now represents a significant foreign policy challenge. Before the window of opportunity closes, an objective reassessment and qualitative change in policy toward the Andean region is urgently needed. Indeed, it is in the fundamental national security interest of the United States to focus attention and action on the Andes, before a regional collapse triggers explosive security and humanitarian crises that demand a far deeper and more politically divisive commitment of U.S. military and financial resources than the U.S. public and Congress can tolerate.[11]

The premise of a new strategy for the Andes is that significantly more investment to build equitable access to markets and jobs,

---

[11]It is important to note that the United States has significant energy interests in the Andes. Between petroleum, natural gas, and coal, the Andean region provides the United States with almost 20 percent of its energy supply, with Venezuela alone providing roughly 14 percent of U.S. oil imports, including a large percentage of the home heating oil used on the East Coast.

sustainable and productive infrastructure, and functioning civil and criminal justice systems is critical for the achievement of sustainable, peaceful democracies—no less than military assistance and drug eradication programs. This strategy recognizes that the region requires both "hard" and "soft" assistance, in the security and socioeconomic arenas, respectively.

Three principles underpin the Commission's work. First is the need for the diffusion of political and economic power in each country in an accountable and democratic fashion, with particular attention paid to integrating the rural areas in this process. Second is the conviction that the United States is a crucial actor in the region, but also that broad and deep engagement on diplomatic, political, economic, social, and humanitarian issues by other international actors—including the UN, the IFIs, regional organizations, and European, Asian, and Latin American countries—is critical. Third is the need for recognition—by the United States, the international community, and the Andean countries themselves—that many of the political, economic, humanitarian, and security problems in the Andes stretch across borders and thereby require strategies that are regional in their approach and implementation.

A new U.S. strategy toward the Andes will necessitate more effective coordination at all levels: between the various agencies of the U.S. government; the United States and the Andean countries (both bilaterally and on a regional basis); and the United States and the other external actors engaged in the Andes. At present, U.S. policy in the Andes—and in Latin America as a whole—seems to be driven by several independently functioning executive branch offices, including the Bureau of International Narcotics and Law Enforcement (INL) at the State Department, the United States Trade Representative (USTR), the Drug Enforcement Administration (DEA), the U.S. Agency for International Development (USAID), and the Department of Defense's U.S. Southern Command (South Com). Unfortunately, each office pursues its agenda in a policy vacuum. As a result, an individual bureaucracy can distort the balance of policy, especially in the absence of more senior-level leadership.

Although an interagency process does exist on specific issues, there appears to be no consistent, senior-level guidance that sets priorities and coordinates the work of various agencies. This type of systematic coordination between U.S. government agencies is urgently needed. The Commission strongly recommends that the national security adviser mandate the creation of an interagency team, headed by the undersecretary for political affairs, to take an objective look at U.S. policy in the Andes. The undersecretary could then deputize, to the level of assistant secretary, the tasks of leveraging multilateral support—particularly from development organizations with a regional focus, such as the Inter-American Development Bank (IDB) and Andean Finance Corporation (Corporación Andina de Fomento, or CAF)—and coordinating action with international partners.

As part of the effort to improve U.S. government coordination on the Andes, it would be useful for the State Department to encourage regular information sharing and discussion meetings among all the U.S. ambassadors in the region. Because ambassadors regularly meet with all the constituent agencies working in the region, these meetings could enable a synthesis of that work, to the benefit of policymakers in Washington. This simple measure currently exists only on an ad hoc basis in the Andes, but it has facilitated an improved "jointness" of strategy in certain instances.

REORIENTING U.S. COUNTERDRUG POLICY

The Commission contends that U.S. drug policy in the Andes excessively emphasizes the supply side of the drug war, especially in the absence of a well-articulated, multilateral effort by the United States and other drug-consuming nations to commit the resources and political capital needed to develop viable economic alternatives for rural farmers involved in cultivating coca and poppy and address the domestic demand side of the problem. Furthermore, as it is currently waged, the efficacy of the United States's supply-side approach is undermined by the absence of effective state sovereignty and law enforcement by local governments.[12] In particular, the emphasis on forced eradication—the aerial spraying of coca crops—is out of sync with reality in rural areas, where there is not an effective state law enforcement "stick" to prevent replanting. At the same time, U.S. efforts to financially decapitate and weaken the narcotrafficking "baby cartels" and their criminal syndicates—including the illegal armed groups—who produce and transport drugs in bulk remain inchoate. Thus, the Commission argues that the U.S. counterdrug policy is flawed in its priorities, allocation of resources, and virtual exclusion of the demand side of the problem.

The Commission therefore recommends a reorientation of U.S. counterdrug policy to emphasize a regional rather than bilateral approach, in recognition of the ease with which drug production crosses borders. It also recommends strategies aimed at the higher strata of the narcotics industry—narcotraffickers and "baby cartels"—with aerial crop eradication being an ongoing but not dominant element;[13] increased funding for—and improved implementation of—rural development strategies to increase the economic incentives for farmers to stop growing coca and poppy; and the multilateralization of responsibility to address the drug war on both the supply and demand sides of the issue.[14]

The current aerial crop eradication program makes inroads in diminishing the amount of coca (the leaf used for cocaine production) cultivated in Peru, Bolivia, and Colombia, but has yet to appreciably impact upon the net combined export of cocaine from these countries.[15] Instead, coca production has spread up and

---

[12]The Commission recognizes that the Colombian government of Alvaro Uribe Vélez and the United States are working to address the issues of insufficient state presence and law enforcement capabilities.

[13]The announcement by the United States and Colombia that aerial interdiction efforts (air bridge denial) to target narcotraffickers will resume is a positive sign for policies directed at the higher strata of the industry.

[14]See the section on U.S. and International Community Engagement, Recommendation 1, of this report for a detailed strategy to multilateralize action against drugs.

[15]As noted below, aerial crop eradication has been at the forefront of U.S. supply-side counterdrug policy since 1999. Under the current administration, there is no evidence that the aerial eradication strategy is losing traction inside the Office of National Drug Control Policy (ONDCP) and the State Department, or that other alternatives are being explored.

down the Andes, indiscriminate of national territory. When coca growing declined in Bolivia and Peru in the 1990s, for example, cultivation and production moved to Colombia. Recently, because of an unprecedented aggressive eradication effort by the Uribe government, coca cultivation fell in Colombia and is expected to have fallen again in 2003, according to U.S. government forecasts. But current trends show that coca cultivation is again on the rise in Bolivia, and there are differing accounts on whether Peru is succeeding in reducing coca levels.[16] At the end of 2002, the net area of land under coca cultivation in the Andes—although lower than the statistics for 2001—was higher than the amount for 2000.[17] Although State Department officials are hopeful that net Andean coca production for 2003 will have fallen below 2000 levels, such a drop would be very difficult to sustain and would still leave approximately 200,000 hectares under cultivation.

Essentially, the United States's counternarcotics bureaucracy has become extremely effective at eradicating coca by country, but not in the region as a whole. Rather, the drug war in the Andes pushes coca and poppy production across borders through vast swaths of territory but has not reduced the region's aggregate supply of cocaine to the United States, nor American demand for drugs.

The underwhelming achievement of coca eradication policy on the ground in the Andes begs two questions: what tools are American policymakers using to break up the narcotrafficking syndicates that control and profit from the drug trade (as opposed to targeting the predominantly poor, rural farmers who grow coca), and what progress, if any, has been made on the other side of the drug war—reducing demand in consuming nations?

With regard to the first question, there have been some U.S.-led efforts to thwart the activities of the estimated eighty-two "baby cartels" operating in and around Colombia: for example, the U.S.

---

[16]"U.S. Says Coca Area Up in Bolivia, Down in Peru," Reuters, November 18, 2003; Hazel Feigenblatt, "Bolivian Growers Increase Their Coca Acreage," *Washington Times,* December 12, 2003.

[17]*International Narcotics Control Strategy Report,* U.S. Department of State, March 2003. Heroin is on the rise throughout the Andes and Colombian-based production is reported to amount for the majority of U.S. consumption of the drug.

DEA publishes a blacklist of Colombian businesses associated with the drug trade, and ongoing efforts are being made to extradite drug traffickers to the United States for trial. However, as compared to the early- to mid-1990s—when breaking up the infamous Medellín and Cali drug cartels was a primary goal of U.S. policy in the region—the narcotrafficking syndicates today receive comparatively little U.S. attention, despite the fact that Colombian cocaine still accounts for 80 percent to 90 percent of the U.S. market. In part, this is due to the complications of the fractured cartel system, which sees a multiplicity of actors—including Colombia's three main illegal armed groups—involved in the drug trade. Nevertheless, an increase in human and financial resources to confront the "baby cartels," with all the levers available to the U.S. government and international community, is merited. Specific measures to this end include empowering the U.S. Treasury Department's Office of Foreign Assets Control (OFAC) to "financially decapitate" the drug cartels by confiscating their holdings in banks and legitimate industries, and increasing earmarked funding assistance to the Colombian government entity (La Dirección Nacional de Estupefacientes) responsible for administering its asset-forfeiture laws.[18]

Meanwhile, the sustainable success of aerial crop eradication efforts is undermined by structural problems of inequality, poverty, and politically disenfranchised rural populations in the Andes. Simply put, eradication will never be completely successful so long as there are poor people on the ground whose only viable option to support themselves and their families is to grow coca or poppy. Accordingly, the Commission strongly recommends increased U.S. funding for, and improved implementation of, economic development and employment programs in rural areas, as part of a broader effort of rural development, land reform, and the extension of state law enforcement presence and social safety nets to the rural areas. Improving the legitimate economic opportunities of

---

[18]See the third section of this report, U.S. and International Community Engagement, for an in-depth recommendation about financial decapitation. In an *El Tiempo* article, entitled "Narco Assets, the Chaos Grows," it is reported that the Colombian government entity responsible for administering the asset-forfeiture laws is understaffed, overburdened, and in near disarray. "Narcobienes, Crece el Caos," *El Tiempo,* June 27, 2003.

the rural poor will be a critical step toward redressing the structural problems that inhibit the efficacy of the current supply-side counternarcotics program.[19]

Regionalizing supply-side efforts—that is, formulating and implementing counterdrug policy on a regional rather than bilateral basis—would improve the effectiveness of U.S. counterdrug activities. The drug industry's ability to operate fluidly across borders is well-established. Working only bilaterally to fight drugs is therefore detrimental to the scope and efficacy of U.S. policy. Additionally, the Commission believes that the drug war will be fought more effectively if other international actors and consuming countries are engaged and encourages the U.S. government to pursue a multilateral approach on non-security-related counterdrug activities.[20]

On the demand side, a historical comparison is useful. Under the Nixon administration, some two-thirds of the U.S. counterdrug budget went to domestic treatment and law enforcement programs and one-third was spent on source-country interdiction programs. During Republican and Democratic administrations in the 1980s and 1990s, this equation was reversed. Focus on supply-side interdiction peaked with the advent of Plan Colombia in 1999, a policy based on aerially eradicating coca and poppy crops. Later, the George W. Bush administration rebalanced the counterdrug funding ratio to reflect a breakdown of 55 percent supply-side and 45 percent demand-reduction, according to its public figures. Still, there is some question as to whether a qualitative shift toward addressing the demand side is occurring. There is currently

---

[19]For more on the specific steps that can be taken to redress structural economic problems, see The Significance of Trade (in Findings, below), with recommendations for direct foreign investment by the manufacturing sector in rural regions and a "strategic preferences regime" for agricultural products facing comparative disadvantages from illicit products and global market trends. See also sections two and three of this report for recommendations on economically engaging excluded populations with robust microfinance initiatives, increased direct investment, and public-private partnerships at local levels; enacting market-based land reform; and making permanent the current trade preference regimes in the Andes in order to boost investor confidence and raise levels of economic activity.

[20]See the third section of this report, U.S. and International Community Engagement, for a specific strategy to multilateralize action on drugs.

no sustained, high-level public awareness and prevention campaign underway to address drug consumption in the United States, nor is there a national effort to address drug addiction from a public health perspective, an idea that some argue could help curb demand.

Secretary of Defense Donald Rumsfeld did recognize the demand side of the drug problem in August 2003, on the eve of his trip to Colombia: "My impression is that, in a very real sense, it's a demand problem. It's a problem that there are a lot of people who want it; a lot of people with money who will pay for it; a lot of people who will steal from others to pay for it. And that you can squeeze it down in one country to zero and you don't change at all the amount of the product that ends up in Europe or the United States because it's demand that determines how much is going to get in there. ... And the higher the price and the greater the willingness of people to take risks, the greater the willingness of people to buy the kinds of things they need to hide what they're doing, and to protect them as they transport these materials. And it's a vicious cycle."[21] Yet this awareness about the importance of the demand side is not adequately reflected in current policy.

The Commission therefore argues that a serious reform strategy for the Andes—one that would significantly reduce the prospect for violent conflict—cannot succeed unless the political leadership and private citizens of the United States support and fund both sustainable demand-reduction programs at home and more varied assistance programs in the Andean region. Because demand drives supply, a counterdrug policy focused solely or predominantly on the supply side of the equation will never fully achieve its goal. Accordingly, the Commission endorses the findings of a 1997 Council on Foreign Relations Task Force report, which argued for increased resources and greater focus on prevention through public education and media campaigns, accessible treatment and rehabilitation, and community law enforcement, as the critical components of a national demand-reduction strategy.[22]

---

[21]Secretary of Defense Donald Rumsfeld, Department of Defense Town Hall Meeting, August 14, 2003.

[22]Mathea Falco et. al., *Rethinking International Drug Control: New Directions for U.S. Policy*, Council on Foreign Relations, 1997.

The United States could indefinitely sustain spending of approximately $1 billion per year on the drug war in the Andes. However, given the region's profound social, economic, and political instability—some of which, as in Bolivia, is directly linked to U.S. drug policy—these resources are being wasted in the absence of a strategy for the region that includes a sustained rural development policy for employment generation, local development initiatives, and land reform; a shift in priorities toward the higher strata of the narcotics industry, with fewer direct effects on poor farmers; increasing coordination and action on counterdrug policy with local and international actors; and demand reduction in the United States, Europe, Brazil, and the Andean region.

ENGAGING THE ENTIRE INTERNATIONAL COMMUNITY

Despite its prominent position in the Andes, the United States does not have the authority or resources to act alone in the region. The United States must take the first step to catalyze the international community to broaden its commitment to the region beyond humanitarian efforts alone. Only through partnership at the international and local levels can the Andean crisis be met with sufficient financial and political resources. Collaboration between a U.S.-led group of principals in the international community—including the UN; European, Asian, and Western Hemisphere partners; and reform-minded Andean governments and their citizens—could produce a bona fide regional strategy founded on the need for economic and rural development, improved rule of law, democratic consolidation, and security requirements beyond the drug war.

The July 2003 London Donor Conference on International Support for Colombia—sponsored by the British government with representation from the United States, Colombia, the UN, the multilateral development community, civil society nongovernmental organizations (NGOs), and nations in Latin America, Europe, and Asia—as well as the multilateral response to Colombia's humanitarian and internally displaced crises now being crafted by the UN, the European Union, the United Kingdom, and Spain highlight a recent increase in involvement by other international actors. However, this positive trend will not produce the necessary results for the region unless the international community is permanently and more broadly engaged. In this respect, the Commission is encouraged that UN Secretary-General Kofi Annan traveled to Ecuador, Peru, and Bolivia in 2003 and has signaled his intention to call a special meeting on the region with all the local heads of state.

THE SIGNIFICANCE OF TRADE

The conventional wisdom that free trade for the Andes will help the region develop market alternatives to coca and poppy byproducts is a sound argument. Both the U.S. International Trade Commission (ITC) and the Congressional Research Services Office reported that intraregional integration and the U.S.-sponsored trade preferences acts—the 1991 Andean Trade Preference Act (ATPA) and its amplified version, the 2002 Andean Trade Promotion and Drug Eradication Act (ATPDEA)—generated higher employment in the Andes.[23] Nevertheless, strategies for sustainable economic growth cannot be divorced from the reality on the ground: the disproportionate comparative advantage for individuals involved in cultivating, producing, or trafficking drugs.

The Commission therefore strongly recommends that the U.S. government coordinate development and trade policies to complement existing alternative development programs administered by USAID and the State Department's INL office. Creating incentives for foreign direct investment and job growth in the rural Andes—particularly in the manufacturing sector, which provides year-round, rather than seasonal, employment and can be a first step to a long-term growth strategy—would greatly increase the likelihood of success for these programs.

---

[23] *The Impact of the Andean Trade Preferences Act*, United States International Trade Commission, September 2002; Raymond J. Ahearn, *Trade and the Americas*, Congressional Research Services Brief for Congress, July 29, 2003.

Within the region, the formation of an Andean customs union with reduced tariff barriers would be a significant incentive for increasing foreign investment and intraregional commerce, and could help diversify rural economies away from the drug industry. Nonetheless, though there have been some signs of reinvigorated political momentum toward trade integration within South America, the Andean governments—with the exception of Venezuela—still believe that their economic and security interests can best be met by pursuing solid bilateral relationships with the United States.[24] There is some merit to this view, and it is certainly logical for the United States to manage and strengthen bilateral security ties while working for a regional cooperation framework. Indeed, as part of a broader strategy for the Andean region, trade is a tool with still-unrealized potential to give the United States powerful leverage for positive change.[25] Just as the United States makes military assistance to Colombia conditional on human rights performance, so can access to U.S. markets through trade serve as a powerful incentive for Andean governments, private sectors, and citizens to make concrete commitments to the rule of law, equitable development, and lasting security.

If the flourishing illegal drug industry is any indication of the region's economic potential, however, the Andes as a whole can best leverage its comparative advantage with the United States and the global economy by acting as a regional unit in trade negotiations for integration with the United States and North America, Mercosur and South America, and an eventual Free Trade Area of the Americas (FTAA). Accordingly, unless explicitly approached as a model for an Andean Free Trade Agreement (AFTA), a bilateral trade agreement between Colombia and the United States

---

[24]Brazil recently decided to grant associate status in Mercosur (the regional trading bloc made up of Brazil, Argentina, Uruguay, and Paraguay, with Bolivia and Chile as associate members) to Peru and, later, Venezuela.

[25]Because of the unequal terms of trade, lack of competitiveness, and poorly developed market infrastructure, many in the region view opening their markets to free trade as a concession to the United States and their neighbors rather than as a benefit to their own economies.

could be highly detrimental to evolving regional relationships, unless it is deliberately crafted as a model for the entire Andean region and broadened quickly to include Ecuador, Peru, Bolivia, and, if desired by its government, Venezuela. A bilateral trade agreement with Colombia alone, without the broader Andean regional initiative underway, could sabotage the incipient cooperation being built by the Uribe government with neighbors on the security front. Such action sends the message that Colombia wants help where it is weak but will leave its neighbors behind where it has comparative strength.

Presently, although the U.S. Trade Representative is doing much of the heavy lifting for U.S. policy in the hemisphere, whether in Central America, Cancún, Brasília, or Bogotá, regional and bilateral trade agreements are not being negotiated within a broader policy context. Although trade policies that are not part of a comprehensive strategic policy may, in fact, provide short-term economic growth, they cannot be expected to reverse the deep-seated structural problems that require a more committed and cohesive approach. Accordingly, it is crucial that the White House, State Department, and Congress act in a more unified manner on trade policy, particularly where trade and development intersect. Washington must also signal to the Andean governments and the local private sector that while free trade talks commence, the United States expects demonstrated progress in establishing and meeting benchmarks for investing in economic development and strengthening the rule of law. For its part, it is crucial that the United States commit to providing adequate adjustment assistance and investment in social protection programs to minimize the negative short-term effects of trade liberalization, upon the enactment of AFTA or the FTAA.

One particular issue of contention with regard to both ATPDEA and potential Andean free trade agreements is whether the United States should grant preferential treatment for strategic agricultural products grown in the drug-producing regions of the Andes. In Colombia, Peru, and Bolivia, where coca growing is based, farmers are moving away from their legitimate traditional cash crops to more productive illicit ones, as a result of economic choice or because of threats of violence and expropriation. Coffee growers, who are confronting a global bean glut and rock-bottom prices for their crop, are especially affected.[26] Advocates of strategic preferences argue that, by pinpointing those sectors of the region's agricultural market most affected by the drug trade and other comparative disadvantages, an improved Andean trade preferences regime could be targeted to specific crops—both as a source of growth for rural populations and as a strategic economic bulwark against illegal armed groups and narcotraffickers who move coca and opium plots into depressed areas.

Implementing an integrated approach—such as the one outlined above, harnessing trade and economic development to combat the effects of the drug industry—would require senior-level U.S. attention to create and institutionalize an interagency process fusing trade, development, and counterdrug efforts within the U.S. government, and to coordinate these activities with the relevant authorities from the Andean governments and the multilateral and NGO development communities.

A New Approach to Colombia

The cornerstone of a new U.S. policy in the Andes must be Colombia, in keeping with current U.S. interests and reflecting the country's importance in the region. At present, the aggressive U.S. policy embodied in Plan Colombia does not enumerate and prioritize the actions, incentives, and resources necessary to move Colombia toward peace. Nor does it plan for a post-conflict, post-drug environment, and the subsequent need to offset the exposure of Colombia's neighbors to the displacement of criminals, narcoterrorists, and guerrillas from its territory. However, past U.S. experience in post-conflict reconstruction demonstrates that a strategy to move Colombia from a seemingly permanent status of

---

[26]Gary Marx, "Coffee Crisis Ravages Colombia; Failing Prices Fuel Coca Production and Civil War," *Chicago Tribune,* April 20, 2003.

internal conflict to a stable democracy with full domestic sovereignty must be holistic.[27]

At the least, moving Colombia toward a sustainable peace will require a combination of enhanced security initiatives beyond counternarcotics; U.S. support for negotiations with and demobilization of all armed groups; a major commitment to addressing the country's rural crisis and lack of infrastructure; promotion of a region-wide Andean trade regime; and border development initiatives for Colombia's north, east, and south. This will necessitate broadening Plan Colombia and the Andean Counterdrug Initiative (ACI) beyond their current focus on the drug war, while preserving, amplifying, and improving, where necessary, the core elements of reinforcing the Colombian armed forces capability and protecting human rights and civil liberties.

On a parallel track, it is appropriate for the United States to explore, with the UN and the Colombian government, how it could best support the negotiation process with the AUC paramilitaries or the FARC and the ELN. The United States has already committed approximately $3 million in assistance for demobilizing AUC paramilitary units.

Although supportive of an ongoing, and hopefully expanded, negotiation process, the Commission is concerned that demobilized combatants who have committed crimes against humanity or violated international law may be allowed to reintegrate into Colombian civil society or, worse, the armed forces, with impunity. Information indicating that paramilitary operatives and drug traffickers either already own, or are engaged in a new round of forced extortion of, much of Colombia's most fertile and valuable

---

[27]In the post–World War II era, the United States fully and successfully grasped the basic political equation that neutralizing one's enemy or consolidating a new democracy requires both "guns and butter." Although the analogy between Colombia today and postwar Germany and Japan is imperfect to say the least, the experience of those countries illustrates a crucial point: the outcome of U.S. efforts at post-conflict reconstruction is largely predicated on whether U.S. policymakers deem those efforts to be in the U.S. national security interest, effectively coordinate the interagency management of a crisis, and invest the necessary resources and time to make the policy a success.

land is also troubling. This process—one that Colombia has experienced before—is known as "reverse land reform."[28] Indeed, paramilitary officials—some of whom are themselves drug traffickers or closely linked to the estimated eighty-two "baby" drug cartels—boast that in the current demobilization talks they have made a priority of maintaining land assets purchased with drug money or extorted from local peasants (who become part of the country's vast internally displaced population).

This depressing phenomenon has obvious adverse effects, such as limiting access to fertile land for agricultural production. Of Colombia's eighteen million hectares of arable land, fewer than four million hectares are being used for agricultural production, with the remaining portion unregistered, protected by rogue interests, or lying fallow.[29] Extortion of land by the FARC and narcotrafficker-AUC alliances can also be correlated to spikes in the levels of violence in particular areas, as a result of the forced displacement that occurs during the land grab.[30] Ill-gotten land that is untaxed and is effectively unproductive for the larger population is desperately needed for any attempt at strategic land reform. Therefore, applying Colombia's asset forfeiture laws to ill-gotten gains now in the hands of any of Colombia's armed actors—for this or any negotiation process—will be critical to a sustainable peace.[31] On a related matter, it is crucial that the Uribe

---

[28]In the mid-1990s, it became apparent that a vast grab of Colombia's most productive land had been orchestrated by the Cali and Medellín cartels and individual paramilitary groups. As a result, accurate statistics of land holdings are extremely difficult to ascertain, and no effective land titling process has been carried out. However, the current research consensus reveals that the reverse land reform process has accelerated and that each illegal armed group owns a significant portion of Colombia's arable land, either through purchasing a counterfeit title, laundering via a third party, or seizing through extortion and force.

[29]Juan Camilo Restrepo, "Tierras sin hombres y hombres sin tierras," *El Tiempo*, January 15, 2003.

[30]Pockets of intense violence are also traceable to areas that fall along strategic routes in the drug trade, where the FARC and the AUC, as well as narcotraffickers and, to a lesser extent, the ELN, face off. Marc Chernick and Alejandro Reyes Posada, *A Methodology for Democratic Conflict Prevention and Early Warning in Latin America: The Case of Colombia*, Georgetown University–UN Development Programme Project on Democracy and Violence, August 2003.

[31]"Narcobienes, crece el caos," *El Tiempo*, June 27, 2003.

administration return land taxing powers to the federal level as part of its effective sovereignty agenda.[32] Under the current system, land taxes—which are administered by municipal authorities under the Colombian constitution of 1991—are practically ignored by landowners, as local governments are often either too weak to exert coercive power over local elite interests or are subject to subornation by an illegal armed group active in the area.

In sum, a fundamental decision is required by the United States: that, in addition to its social and economic benefits, legal land reform in Colombia—rather than a land grab at gunpoint—is a critical strategic imperative, and must be a top priority on the agendas of the United States and international community in their dealings with Colombia.[33]

The Commission is concerned that the demands of fighting a war on two or three fronts, as well as the understandable reluctance to appear to make any concessions to enemy groups, have prevented the Colombian government from laying the groundwork for a sustainable postwar environment. Nor does it appear that the United States is pushing for such planning. In part, it seems, the Colombian government is reluctant to undertake strategic planning for the country's rural crisis—or for establishing legitimate state institutions other than for security—on the grounds that such action will legitimize the historic ideological demands for land reform and political inclusion by the armed, now narcoterrorist-infused groups.

This self-defeating dynamic must stop. There can be no lasting security in Colombia's vast territory, including on the country's five borders, without social and development programs—encompassing land reform—for the poor and excluded, and expanded access to justice, markets, and political participation. In other words, although Colombia must confront the military threat posed by the illegal armed groups with force, it must also address

---

[32]The Commission takes a practical approach to the issue of decentralization, identifying instances where it is appropriate or imprudent because of poor security conditions or because of the need for federal-level political leadership.

[33]In April 2002, the Uribe government gave the titles to 5,600 hectares of land seized from drug traffickers to 450 peasant families. An additional 314,000 hectares are being processed under the country's asset forfeiture laws. *El Tiempo*, September 1, 2003.

the nation's insidious problems in rural areas through innovative economic development, strategic land reform, and building political institutions. Each of these objectives will be achieved in part by reining in rogue local and regional actors who undermine state initiatives.

Despite the current administration's popularity, and the unprecedented political will in support of its "democratic security" approach, the Uribe government still lacks the political leverage to reverse Colombia's historically weak state institutions. This factor clearly inhibits the government's ability to make essential strategic reforms, as evidenced by the failure of the Uribe government–sponsored referendum on political and fiscal reform in October 2003. The United States and the international community could play an invaluable role in assisting the Uribe administration on these matters if both sides recognize the need for domestic reforms. Greater international attention and carefully managed political support would strengthen Uribe's hand in convincing local political and financial elites that these reforms are needed to construct a legitimate state with effective sovereignty, and in surmounting the anti-reformist machinations of rogue Colombian elements. Without explicit pressure from the international community for Colombia to simultaneously address these integrated threats, it is likely that the emphasis on force over development will continue to prevail.

Fortunately, Colombians seem increasingly open to considering the far-reaching changes necessary to end the conflict and achieve a sustainable peace. It is imperative that the United States encourage this trend and, in so doing, make use of the fact that the Colombian government and armed forces are acutely sensitive to, and accommodating of, Washington's emphasis on the war on drugs and the war on terror. At present, the U.S. government is constructively engaging Uribe on the importance of security and the drug war, striking at the most pressing and prevalent threats but excluding the fundamental issues for long-term peace building. This policy is expedient, and it satisfies constituencies in both Colombia and Washington who would rather not invest in development and land reform initiatives, but it is incomplete and undermines the

Successes and Shortcomings of Plan Colombia

The Commission considers the three fundamental flaws of current U.S. policy in the Andes, as embodied in Plan Colombia, to be a narrow focus on counternarcotics and security issues, with insufficient attention to other equally pressing priorities; a lack of substantive participation and assistance by other international actors; and unanticipated detrimental regional effects—including migration of guerrillas, arms, drugs, and narcotraffickers throughout the Andes—that are not countered by positive, regionally oriented strategies. These defects narrow the scope and effectiveness of U.S. policy to the detriment of a comprehensive strategy for the multitude of interrelated problems in the region. On the positive side, however, Plan Colombia has eradicated coca bushes in southern Colombia, helped install measures to decrease human rights violations by the Colombian armed forces, stabilized Colombia's democracy, and provided a foundation for the U.S. government to launch what has become an important, long-term strategic endeavor for the Andes.

Plan Colombia was crafted in 1999 at a moment of crisis: the Colombian economy had suffered its first contraction of GDP in decades; the size and power of the country's illegal armed groups continued to grow; the drug trade persisted; the armed forces were underfunded and low in morale; and citizens in Bogotá and other major cities were personally affected by terrorism for almost the first time. The policy began the process of professionalizing the Colombian armed forces and eradicating coca and, to a lesser extent, poppy. It also launched the United States into an important nation building role in the country. Concomitant funds from the ACI, along with additional resources to train Colombian forces to protect the Ecopetrol–Occidental Petroleum–Repsol YPF jointly owned Caño Limon–Covenas pipeline in eastern Colombia—and, more recently, flexibility to use U.S. funds, equipment, and American-trained Colombian brigades to fight drugs and illegal armed groups—solidified that role. Colombia is now the third largest recipient of U.S. aid and the U.S. embassy in Bogotá has the largest staff of any American diplomatic mission in the world.

The investment in Plan Colombia is producing impressive results within the confines of its intended scope. According to the State Department, over 50 percent of coca hectares under cultivation in 2000 will have been eradicated well before the stated goal of 2005, and the Colombian brigades trained by U.S. Special Forces and vetted for human rights standards under the plan are widely regarded as models of professionalism.

Nevertheless, endemic problems—including violations of human rights and international humanitarian law, impunity, corruption, poverty, inequality, violent crime, and chronic insecurity—persist. Furthermore, an unintended consequence of Plan Colombia has been the reduced participation of European partners and multilateral institutions in shared efforts to address the root causes of instability in the region. Several factors played a role in the relative marginalization of other international actors in the Andes. At the time of Plan Colombia's creation, the European Commission and relevant UN entities (such as the UN Development Programme) objected to its content—an overarching focus on crop eradication, interdiction, and security assistance—and its process, which they felt was carried out with insufficient consultation with allies. Subsequently, the EU, Japan, and the UN largely went their own way in the Andes, focusing on small, discrete development activities outside the context of Plan Colombia.[34]

The U.S. government's security-centric strategy neglects the fact that the illicit economies and industries in the region take advantage of the institutional weaknesses of states and the self-interest of traditional elites. The majority of elites in Colombia and across the Andean region have not used their influence to pressure the national or local authorities to establish legitimate institutions of law enforcement, public security, infrastructure, and basic social welfare throughout the country's vast territory. For example, although revenue from taxes in Colombia has risen from 10 to 13 percent of GDP since 2000, it remains an embarrassing fact that only 740,000 Colombians pay income tax in a country of 42 million people (a problem the Uribe government has now recognized and is attempting to combat by cracking down on evasion and passing measures to induce greater contribution).[35] Income tax revenue in the rest of the region is also low.[36] On the other hand, the United States recently reported that the amount of money laundered in Colombia reached $5 billion in 2002. Plan Colombia was not designed to reverse this trend. Yet without such a reversal, sustainable progress on all fronts—political, economic, and security—is unfeasible.

[34]Since the September 11, 2001, attacks, the distance between the United States and Europe with respect to the Andes has begun to narrow, as evidenced by the U.K.-hosted Donor Conference on International Support for Colombia held in July 2003, and by the participation of the UN, the EU, Chile, Brazil, Mexico, Japan, and Spain in devising an international response to Colombia's humanitarian crisis. See Engaging the Entire International Community, in the Findings section of this report. See also Joaquin Roy, *European Perceptions of Plan Colombia: A Virtual Contribution to a Virtual War and Peace Plan?* North-South Center, May 2001.

[35]A partial exception is last year's one-time wealth tax, which provided approximately $700 million in revenues (equal to 0.5 percent of GDP) for security assistance—a substantial percentage of which was contributed by a handful of wealthy Colombian citizens. Juan Forero, "Burdened Colombians Back Tax to Fight Rebels," *New York Times*, September 8, 2002.

[36]See Appendix B for information on revenue from taxes in the Andes.

incipient creative thinking and problem-solving capability in the Uribe administration.

No one disputes the significance of establishing security and state presence throughout the country, or the correlation between achieving good results on the security front and the ability to actually implement economic development programs, strategic land reform, and political institution-building projects. However, only with more robust engagement and political support from the United States, the EU, and the international community on the need for social and political reform in Colombia will current and future administrations be able to embrace and implement a comprehensive policy agenda.

BEYOND COLOMBIA: THE CHALLENGES TO ECUADOR AND VENEZUELA

Ecuador and Venezuela—the other two countries of focus for this report—are not faced by the prospect of illegal armed groups waging conflict against their elected governments, but their respective political landscapes are far from tranquil. With a similar history of exclusionary politics, woefully inadequate property and income tax collection, banking crises, rampant corruption, opaque financial accounts, and cyclical political strife, Ecuador and Venezuela's political and social instability could easily threaten the region as a whole.

Ecuador, a country of twelve million people with a modest economy,[37] experienced habitual periods of political, economic, and social upheaval in the last five years. The current president, Lucio Gutiérrez, is an army colonel who served time in jail for his participation in a coup in 2000. His government was the first in Ecuadoran history to include representatives of the country's indigenous population in the cabinet, although that alliance ended due to a variety of policy disagreements. Although elected with a limited mandate, Gutiérrez implemented a domestically unpopular Inter-

---

[37]The size of Ecuador's economy is estimated at $24.2 billion.

national Monetary Fund (IMF) program geared toward recovering fiscal stability and solvency after a sequence of banking crises, a loan default, and dollarization plunged the country into virtual insolvency and ungovernability in the late 1990s.

At any given time, President Gutiérrez faces destabilizing political and social conflict from a variety of sources, including his own cabinet members; indigenous groups; the country's regionally based political actors; the financially powerful coastal elites of Guayaquil; opposition parties in the Congress; the armed forces; and opponents of the IMF program from left, right, or indigenous groups. A disabled judiciary, widespread corruption, and entrenched extortionist political behavior of some in the ancien régime also pose significant structural impediments that make governing difficult for any Ecuadoran president, regardless of the size of his mandate. As of December 2003, President Gutiérrez's popularity ratings were at their lowest point yet—down from 56 percent to 18 percent—as a result of a congressional investigation into allegations that he accepted drug money during his election campaign.

Oil, bananas, cut flowers, and remittances are the main sources of revenue for Ecuador's dollarized economy. The oil and banana sectors, in particular, are associated with some of the country's most prominent social and political problems. For example, almost half of Ecuador's annual $3 billion in oil revenues is untraceable through government accounts; while a dispute over value-added tax (VAT) repayment to the consortium of U.S. and other foreign companies that invested in a new oil pipeline is currently holding up operations at the cost of significant losses in revenue. Indigenous groups are also challenging foreign petroleum companies over alleged environmental contamination by the industry and questioning the government's decision to aggressively explore drilling and extraction of oil resources from the Amazonian basin region for future development initiatives. Additionally, the military's involvement in the oil and other industries, both as a beneficiary of the revenues and an arbiter of foreign investment, is problematic.

Unlike oil—which is more important as a source of income than employment—the Ecuadoran banana industry is a significant source of jobs and provides 24 percent of U.S. banana consumption and 21 percent of European banana consumption. However, the structure of the banana industry is both highly inefficient and unequal. The industry accounts for serious human rights violations—including child labor, denial of collective bargaining rights, and union representation—and nominal provision of social security benefits to workers.[38] Although neither representatives of banana workers, nor owners or exporters, want to see a boycott of Ecuadoran bananas, the international community has yet to devise a credible instrument for obliging the banana business to implement either Ecuador's own labor codes or those of the International Labor Organization (ILO). Although the banana industry may commit in principle to honor domestic and international labor rights, the ineffectiveness of the country's court system remains a serious impediment to tangible enforcement, thus raising the question of whether the threat of loss to the U.S. market (and ATPDEA benefits) might encourage improvements in labor rights.

In Venezuela, President Hugo Chávez has missed the opportunity to channel his significant popular mandate of 1998 and 2000 into programs to diversify the economy and democratize the country's political institutions.[39] (Like President Gutiérrez, President Chávez was also briefly imprisoned following a failed coup attempt in 1992, before being elected to the presidency in 1998.) However, by actively supporting the April 2002 coup attempt against Chávez, some in the disorganized opposition appear to have squandered the political capital of the opposition's legitimate democratic forces, both at home and with the international community. As a result of political, social, and economic mismanagement, poverty and inequality are worsening, capital flight is rampant, public security is deteriorating, and Venezuela's standing within

---

[38] *Ecuador: Escalating Violence Against Banana Workers*, Human Rights Watch, May 22, 2002; Juan Forero, "In Ecuador's Banana Fields, Child Labor Is Key to Profits," *New York Times*, November 24, 2002.

[39] Venezuela is significantly larger than Ecuador in terms of its population and economy, with an estimated 24 million people and GDP of $91.5 billion, much of it coming from oil.

the Andean region and with the United States has declined precipitously.[40]

Since the coup attempt of April 2002, the international community's effort to mediate a solution in Venezuela has been led by the secretary-general of the Organization of American States (OAS), César Gaviria. The United States has yet to find its proper role in committing Venezuela's political actors, both government and the opposition, to a constitutional, democratic, and electoral solution to the country's current impasse, in part because the Bush administration did not immediately and firmly condemn the April 2002 coup attempt. Although bilateral drug control cooperation continues, high-level military-to-military contacts have ended, leaving U.S. energy companies as some of the principal interlocutors with the Venezuelan government.

Venezuela's nonenergy private sector is weak compared to Colombia's, but it is playing an important role in the current political impasse. In the wake of a December 2002 national strike led by the Venezuelan business association and labor movement—in which oil production was briefly cut off—the Chávez administration has implemented currency controls. These controls purportedly protect currency against a run on revenues, but they have been used to punish those companies and individuals associated with anti-Chávez activities. The reputation of Venezuela in Washington is further diminished by the growing influence of the Cuban government on the programs and policies of the Chávez government. Without a solution to the political polarization in the country, the Commission is increasingly pessimistic about Venezuela's future.

The Chávez government's credibility in the international community will rise or fall on the basis of whether it facilitates or blocks a constitutional provision allowing a national referendum on the presidency. There is significant cause for concern that President Chávez will delay that democratic process until it is in his interest to go forward with a general election. As of December 2003,

---

[40]According to PROVEA, the leading Venezuelan human rights organization, approximately 150 Venezuelans are killed each weekend, victims of common crime.

both the OAS and the U.S.-based Carter Center, which are observing the recall process, indicated that the referendum process was proceeding in a democratic and fair fashion, although with scattered reports of political violence.[41]

Although Ecuador and Venezuela's problems may seem common to developing nations—and their rogue actors and illegal industries are not nearly as powerful as the narcotraffickers and illegal armed groups in neighboring Colombia—the political trends in both countries allow no room for complacency. Despite, or perhaps because of, their histories of extraconstitutional changes in government, significant portions of the populations in these two nations still demonstrate a disregard for constitutional norms and processes: Venezuela experienced failed coup attempts in 1992 and 2002, Ecuador a successful one in 2000. Venezuelans are deeply polarized over the rule of President Chávez and, ominously, government supporters and detractors have armed themselves, in fear that they cannot trust their government for security in the event that civil strife erupts. The political situation in Ecuador has not escalated to that dangerous level, but Ecuadorans admit that President Gutiérrez's administration could become untenable if fiscal stability breaks down and popular discontent swells up in a form similar to the mass demonstrations that precipitated the 2000 coup. Simply put, the United States cannot discount the collapse of democracy and outbreak of deadly violence in either Ecuador or Venezuela—a development that would have severe implications for U.S. policy and regional stability.

STRATEGIC OBJECTIVES FOR THE REGION

The Commissions' findings, as outlined above, point to the need for a significant departure from current policy in the Andes. In the following chapters, the Commission sets forth specific recommendations in support of a new policy for conflict prevention, based

---

[41]Scott Wilson, "Venezuelan Petition Drive Fair, Observers Say," *Washington Post,* December 2, 2003.

on three mutually reinforcing objectives. First is the need for a major investment of financial and political resources in the rural regions of the Andean nations—by far the areas that are poorest, most excluded, and most vulnerable to violent conflict. Second is the paramount importance of broader and committed engagement by the United States and the international community on the gamut of issues at play in the Andes, in particular the multilateralization of the drug war on both the demand and supply sides. Third is the fact that truly regional problems of security, economic development, and the rule of law and democratic consolidation require that regional solutions be crafted and implemented by the United States, the international community, and Andean actors.

Three sets of recommendations follow: rural development and land reform; U.S. and international community engagement on strategic humanitarian, security, development, and diplomatic issues; and regional approaches to regional problems. Following these primary recommendations are a set of supplementary recommendations that are more technical in nature.

LAND REFORM AND RURAL DEVELOPMENT

Many inhabitants of the rural areas of the Andes are trapped in a cycle of poverty, inequality, and exclusion from economic and social resources. The situation in these areas is acute and has destabilizing political, economic, humanitarian, and security ramifications. For example, the widespread lack of opportunity in licit industries, coupled with enduring economic instability, complicates domestic and international efforts to eradicate coca and break the tenacious grip of the narcotics industry. At the same time, the persistence of wide swaths of territory with a nominal or nonexistent state presence exemplifies rural populations' disenfranchisement and vulnerability to violence and criminality.

At present, none of the Andean countries has devised, much less funded and implemented, cohesive and comprehensive policies for the political and economic integration of the majority of their rural populations. Yet the Andean region's security and prosperity will continue to be undermined unless a concerted strategy is undertaken to commit the resources of Andean governments, the United States, and other international partners toward investment in the rural sector. The current emphasis on alternative development as a complement to domestically unpopular aerial crop eradication and spraying activities in coca growing areas is also unlikely to be effective in the absence of a broader economic strategy for rural regions.

Priorities for a rural strategy include poverty reduction, land reform, infrastructure development, the creation of legitimate economic opportunities in agriculture and industry, and expanded market access and political inclusion. Making progress on these priorities will ease the plight of rural citizens, reduce poverty, and enable the Andean countries to take full advantage of the benefits of regional, and eventually hemispheric, integration.

The Commission recognizes that there are obstacles that limit the capacity of Andean governments to invest sufficiently in the rural sector. These include physical insecurity and, in some areas, lack of effective state sovereignty, constrained fiscal resources, ballooning public debt, and inadequate tax revenue. Nonetheless, the lack of coordinated, dedicated planning for rural development by regional governments, the United States, international organizations, and other external players does nothing to alleviate these problems and, in fact, may compound them.

Accordingly, the Commission argues that the sizable U.S. investments in Andean alternative agricultural development started under the Andean Counterdrug Initiative (ACI) can no longer be effectively implemented independent of the World Bank, the Inter-American Development Bank (IDB), and local initiatives for poverty reduction, decentralization, and institutional reform in the rural sector. The multilateral development community's poverty reduction strategies for rural sectors can be linked with Andean and U.S. government-led efforts on the political integration, governance, and security fronts.

The following recommendations are therefore addressed to both Andean and external players, including the governments, international organizations, and the international financial institutions (IFIs).

1. *Impose and Enforce Property Taxes and Penalize Evasion with the Clearing of Land Titles.* No one has the right to own land without paying property taxes. Rather, societies in which property owners are required to pay taxes on real estate evolve over time into societies in which land ownership is widely distributed, since market principles begin to operate once taxes are levied in a predictable and equitable fashion. In support of this principle—which carries with it the opportunity for strengthening government regulatory and enforcement institutions through increased revenues—the Commission recommends linking the expansion of property rights to the establishment of real property taxes, property tax payment, and collection enforcement. This requires a twofold process: the imposition of a stricter collection regime for property tax, and the institution of a process for clearing title of land abandoned

by owners, whereby those who work the land receive title after an established period of nonpayment of taxes by absentee owners.

The Commission recognizes that this recommendation will be controversial among landowners and potentially open to bureaucratic abuse. Accordingly, it is necessary that a grace period of up to a year is provided before beginning the escheat of property, during which time the process of tax collection can be improved. Several agencies within the U.S. Treasury Department—including the Internal Revenue Service's Office of Tax Administration Advisory Services, the Customs Service, and the Office of Technical Assistance—can provide training and technical advice on tax collection issues and procedures, as can the newly established International Law Enforcement Academy (ILEA) in San Jose, Costa Rica. The Inter-American Center of Tax Administrations (CIAT), which receives partial financing from the IDB, also provides training, technical assistance, and information to its member tax administrations (including those of all Andean countries). At the cessation of the grace period, the process of title forfeiture for nonpayment of taxes can begin.

An obvious incentive for the Andean countries to improve tax policy and enforcement is the prospect of increased government revenues. The U.S. government can also encourage the reform process by linking the necessary domestic policy reforms to trade incentives and U.S. aid for rural programs, and by using its authority to withhold visas and freeze bank accounts of egregious tax evaders (as determined by the home country, not the United States).

2. *Accelerate Land Titling and Registry.* Establishing and enforcing a real property tax regime is only a first, albeit vital, step toward broadening land ownership in the Andes. This is important because lack of access to land title makes it difficult for people—often poor peasants—to secure credit and participate in the market economy. To rectify this situation, and complement the recommendation above, it is necessary to design and implement land administration programs that ensure the registration of secure

land titles; improve demarcation systems; and make a concerted effort to establish fair and accurate appraisals of land values. With the assistance of the World Bank, Peru and Bolivia have such programs up and running, and the Commission encourages Colombia and Ecuador to follow suit. The Commission further recommends that new U.S. foreign aid assistance be conditioned on progress in creating a more equitable and secure distribution of land.

3. *Prioritize Transparent and Accountable Land Reform.* With systematic and credible land titling and demarcation systems in place, other land reform options can be explored. These efforts will require technical and financial assistance from multilateral institutions. Equally important, they will necessitate recognition of and clear signaling by the United States that land reform is a strategic issue that is critical to sustainable development and security in the region. It is therefore important to organize the financing and technical groundwork for ambitious, lawful, and transparent efforts to rectify inequalities in land ownership.[42]

In Ecuador, Peru, and Bolivia, options for substantive land reform include experimentation with market-assisted land reform programs—in consultation with the World Bank and other qualified institutions—that would enhance the negotiating power of poor households to purchase high quality land and provide the credit and other resources needed to make that land productive. In Colombia, meanwhile, the government

---

[42]Brazil has the most unequal land distribution in South America, with 20 percent of the population owning 90 percent of all arable land and the poorest 40 percent owning only 1 percent. However, the experience of Brazil's engagement with the World Bank in pursuing market-assisted land reform in its northeast region is instructive for the Andean community nations. The political will demonstrated by the Fernando Henrique Cardoso administration in the 1990s to request technical and administrative assistance from the World Bank, and the current efforts to advance the land reform process by the administration of Luiz Inacio "Lula" da Silva, is a model of the presidential initiative needed to tackle a contentious issue like land reform. According to the World Bank, Brazil is the only government in South America that has requested technical and administrative assistance for such a program.

can accelerate the redistribution of prime agricultural land seized under streamlined asset forfeiture laws to internally displaced persons (IDPs) and other landless peasants. On this specific point, the U.S. government can earmark funding to the Colombian Dirección Nacional de Estupefacientes (DNE), the government entity responsible for administering the asset forfeiture laws, which, according to the Colombian Contraloría (the equivalent of the U.S. General Accounting Office), is understaffed and operates inefficiently. Funding would be directed toward capacity building for the DNE and would help expedite the processing and redistribution of land titles.[43] Additional technical support from, and political pressure by, the United States would be required to bring this program to fruition.

Furthermore, as noted in the Findings section of this report, it is vital for the Uribe government to halt the ongoing land grab by the paramilitaries. If this "off-the-books" action continues unchecked, the current opportunity for sustainable and strategic land reform in Colombia may evaporate. Unfortunately, the Colombian government lacks sufficiently strong domestic law enforcement and judicial institutions to effectively stem opportunistic land grabs by paramilitaries, drug cartels, or the Revolutionary Armed Forces of Colombia (FARC) or the National Liberation Army (ELN). The Commission therefore recommends that the U.S. government publicly outline a two-tiered policy designed to assist the Colombian government in actualizing sustainable and strategic land reform. The first element would be the publication by the U.S. Drug Enforcement Administration (DEA) of a roster of illegally held and ill-gotten lands and their holders, as part of a public shaming campaign led by the U.S. ambassador. This roster would be analogous to the U.S. government's list of Colombian businesses prohibited from investing in, or forming partnerships with, U.S. entities because of their links to the narcotics or other illegal industries. Cooperation from Bogotá on this matter would be vital.

---

[43]"Narcobienes, crece el caos," *El Tiempo*, June 27, 2003.

The second element of the policy would focus on the actual implementation of land reform. The Commission recommends that the U.S. government provide its own senior-level task force to assist in the technical and legal issues involved in this reform. It also advocates enlisting technical and financial support from the Food and Agriculture Organization (FAO) of the United Nations and other relevant multilateral agencies.

In Venezuela, a program of land reform and property titling is already underway. On paper, this program consists of taxing large holdings that lie idle, and creating mechanisms for redistribution of government-owned and fallow land to small-scale producers. Although the Commission applauds efforts at sustainable, transparent land reform, it is troubled by recent allegations of illegal expropriation and by the potential for conflict as a result of such actions.[44] Accordingly, we strongly recommend that the Hugo Chávez government avoid tacit or overt approval of low-intensity conflict between the landless peasants (*campesinos*) and the wealthy landowners and their hired agents. Thus, as a means of adding legitimacy to—and ensuring the objectivity of—its land reform initiative, the Commission recommends that the government of Venezuela seek technical assistance from the FAO and other relevant multilateral agencies to review land titles and landholdings; update disputed records and define what is considered "unproductive land"; and demonstrate a long-term commitment to its urban and rural land reform programs by providing credit, capital, and technical support programs to new title holders.

4. *Finance Trust Funds for Andean Rural Development.* U.S. financial commitment specifically targeted to rural issues is crucial to the effective implementation and eventual success of development strategies in the Andes. The Commission therefore recommends that the United States establish trust funds at the Andean Finance Corporation (Corporación Andina de Fomento, or CAF) and/or the IDB, to make grants available

---

[44]For an informative account of the battle over land reform in Venezuela, see Reed Lindsay, "Land Reform in Venezuela," *Toronto Star*, September 21, 2003.

to Andean member countries for land reform and other structural reforms that create better economic opportunities for the rural poor. Housing the trust funds at regional organizations would leverage the existing capabilities, relationships, and expertise in the area. To ease potential U.S. concerns about how the money is spent, however, the funds could be structured to require U.S. approval of actual commitments. A matching requirement—whereby Andean governments must match new U.S. commitments with their own funds—could potentially be included to further oblige Andean governments to dedicate their own resources to rural economic development and social and legal reform. The matching requirement would also reinforce the importance of generating new revenues from tax collection and could be phased in to allow this capacity to be further developed.

5. *Focus New Rural Investments on Infrastructure and Local Public-Private Partnerships.*

Invest in Infrastructure. Critically needed basic infrastructure—including roads, electricity, schools, health posts, sewage, and potable water sources—is required to unleash the productive capacity of rural areas. Short-term investments in these areas would also create jobs and strengthen the capacity of local governments and community organizations. Such projects are already a central part of U.S. Agency for International Development (USAID) programs in the Andean region, but they are vastly underfunded. Given the important employment and development needs that infrastructure investment fills, the Commission recommends that a higher priority be assigned to sustainable infrastructure projects by USAID and other bilateral and multilateral donors.

Facilitate Local Public-Private Partnerships. Because of the current low capacity of local governments to generate resources and collect taxes, local governments are largely dependent on resource flows from the central government for revenues. Private-public partnerships can help boost fiscal revenues at the local level. The European Commission and World

Bank–funded Magdalena de Medio "Peace Laboratory" project in Colombia and the Yungas Community Development Investment Fund in Bolivia (initiated by USAID) are examples of successful community-driven development programs that combine domestic finance with international assistance and reward local initiative.

The private sector is crucial here. Rather than simply investing resources in public relations–driven philanthropic initiatives, companies—particularly extractive companies active in the rural sectors—can be encouraged by the United States and other actors, especially nongovernmental organizations (NGOs), to undertake broader development projects coordinated with national and local governments. By harnessing and leveraging the resources of the private sector, this approach would result in significant change at the local level without requiring large international investment.

6. *Mobilize Microfinance to Convert the Informal Sector into a Genuine Private Sector of Small and Medium-Sized Businesses.* Economic diversification and the development of a small and medium-sized business sector are critical to an effective rural strategy. Since as much as 50 percent of Andean economic activity occurs in the informal sector, the potential economic and social benefits, and profitability, of microfinance are unrealized. Through USAID, the United States can increase its current levels of assistance to microfinance institutions (MFIs), focusing on organizations with proven track records and financial self-sustainability. This investment can be complemented by technical assistance to small and medium-sized enterprises, designed to facilitate effective marketing in both local and, where applicable, regional and global markets. Efforts in these areas have proven effective in reducing poverty and raising living standards. MFI success stories—such as those supported by the CAF, Banco Solidario in Bolivia, Compartamos in Mexico, BanGente in Venezuela, Banco Solidario in Ecuador, and Mibanco in Peru—are models for best practices, though

it is important that MFIs are supervised by the relevant domestic regulator.

7. *Procure and Coordinate Targeted Funding for Rural Development Initiatives from Regional and International Financial Institutions.* A new interagency group based on a partnership of major multilateral agencies and key bilateral donors, including the United States and the European Union, has been created at IDB to serve as a coordinating mechanism for rural development in Latin America. The Commission recommends that the interagency group establish a working committee specifically for the Andean region, through which high-level representatives from the multilateral and bilateral agencies can organize and direct new investments and approaches with a timetable that sets clear goals to be achieved in the next year. A parallel committee could be established through the Andean Community's Secretariat, as a forum for Andean governments to address their shared challenges and for multilateral and bilateral actors to engage with regional issues. The interagency group could play a critical role in formulating projects to deal with the challenges presented by border regions.

Tackling the problems of border regions is particularly challenging because the multilateral agencies that provide the bulk of foreign financing for investment in underserved regions—particularly the World Bank—typically fund only national, rather than regional, projects, and are therefore not organized to address political and economic challenges that cross borders. Within the World Bank's institutional framework, however, it is important that the individual governments actively engage to raise funds to complement U.S. and multilateral investments in the rural Andes.[45] Specifically, the Commission rec-

---

[45]In Latin America, the Andean region holds the distinction of being the area with the largest gap between demonstrated needs and current World Bank spending. Of the Andean countries, only Bolivia is eligible for International Development Association (IDA) concessionary loans and grants. Because they are "middle income" countries, Colombia, Venezuela, Ecuador, and Peru do not receive the most generous terms and conditions for World Bank funding.

ommends that the new country assistance strategies (CAS) negotiated between the World Bank and the individual
governments include loan commitments that prioritize investment in the rural sector.[46]

Parallel loans to neighboring governments, or efforts to
fund binational initiatives to shore up local governments, repair
infrastructure, and promote economic development in border
regions, will also be required to ensure that capacity-building
in one country is not offset by neglect in another. New
economic and sector work (ESW)—the World Bank's
analytical program—can focus on how best to channel new
international and domestic resources to address issues in rural
development.

---

[46]The CAS is the central vehicle for Board review of the World Bank Group's assistance strategy for IDA and International Bank for Reconstruction and Development (IBRD)
borrowers. The CAS document describes the World Bank Group's strategy based on an
assessment of priorities in the country and indicates the level and composition of assistance to be provided based on the strategy and the country's portfolio performance. The
CAS is prepared with the government in a participatory way, and its key elements are
discussed with the government prior to Board consideration. However, it is not a negotiated document. Any differences between the country's own agenda and the strategy advo-
cated by the World Bank are highlighted in the CAS document. See www.worldbank.org.

U.S. AND INTERNATIONAL
COMMUNITY ENGAGEMENT

A central premise of this report is that the United States is the major international actor in the Andes, but that it is in the interests of Washington and the region to actively seek substantive engagement by other external players—including the United Nations, the international financial institutions (IFIs), regional organizations, and European, Asian, and American partners—on strategic, diplomatic, development, and humanitarian issues. Simply put, the scale of the crisis in the Andean region requires concerted action from the entire spectrum of the international community. Ensuring that the response to the multitude of challenges facing the Andes is multilateral would increase the resources and capacity being channeled into the region; amplify the incentives for Andean governments to implement needed reforms; and undermine the populist, anti-American rhetoric often employed by governments or opposition members to justify resistance to economic and political changes.

The recommendations that follow are therefore targeted to the international community, including the United States, and offer strategies for how a wide range of external actors can most constructively engage with the Andean states. A multilateral approach is encouraged wherever possible, particularly in the fight against drugs (including demand reduction in consuming countries); efforts to stimulate economic growth and development; and the response to the humanitarian crisis of refugees and internally displaced persons (IDPs).[47]

But multilateralism is not, of itself, a panacea. To be effective, it is necessary that international action be coordinated and cohesive, undertaken in consultation with local governments and other

---

[47]Multilateral approaches to rural development are addressed in the previous section of this report.

key constituencies, and pegged to clear, common goals. Furthermore, not all challenges lend themselves to a multilateral approach. Security assistance is a pertinent example. The United States is the primary source of military and security assistance to the region (particularly Colombia) for a variety of reasons and this state of affairs is unlikely to change in the near future.[48] Accordingly, most of the security-focused recommendations that follow are narrowly targeted toward the U.S. government.

American security assistance to Colombia and the region is a contentious issue for Europe and is commonly cited as a barrier to multilateralizing aid and engagement. However, since the collapse of former president Andres Pastrana's peace negotiations with the Revolutionary Armed Forces of Colombia (FARC) in February 2001, the numerous terrorist attacks by illegal armed groups in Colombian cities, and the events of September 11, 2001, the divide between the United States and Europe on the need for security assistance has narrowed. The time has come, therefore, for the United States and Europe to work together—with international organizations and other partners—to forge a new consensus on a multilateral policy toward Colombia and the Andes: an approach that treats security and counterdrug issues on par with structural problems related to economic development, the rule of law, democracy consolidation, and humanitarian and rural crises.

MULTILATERALIZE ACTION ON DRUGS AND DEVELOPMENT

1. *Broaden International Action against Drugs.* The tactics, implementation, and ramifications of the United States's war

---

[48]With the partial exception of the United Kingdom, France, and Spain, bilateral or multilateral European assistance to Latin America is strictly non-military. Notwithstanding the capacity (or lack thereof) of European states to conduct security assistance programs in the Andes, it is unlikely that their individual political and economic interests would dictate that they do so. The lack of a NATO equivalent in Latin America further shifts responsibility for military reform and professionalization tasks (such as those undertaken by NATO's Partnership for Peace program and Membership Action Plan) onto the United States.

on drugs in the Andes provoke controversy in both the region and the U.S. homeland and have had a chilling effect on the participation of other international actors—particularly the European states—in fighting drugs and illegal industries in the Andes. Although many European states view the drug war through a public health lens, this does not absolve them of active engagement in addressing the scourge of drugs in the Andes, particularly as demand for illegal drugs is growing on both sides of the Atlantic.

The Commission believes that the pernicious effects of illegal drugs—in both producing and consuming countries—will be combated more effectively through a multifaceted, multilateral approach that combines financial incentives, broadly based international participation and pressure, and shared responsibility on both the supply and demand sides of the problem. Indeed, finding points of consensus for addressing the global nature of demand for illegal drugs is crucial to broadening overall international engagement and support for the Andes.

The Commission therefore recommends the following. First, endow the UN Office on Drugs and Crime (UNODC) with the necessary authority to be the primary international monitor of drug production, trafficking, and consumption, responsible for producing reliable statistics based on available data and satellite imagery. Once solid statistics are obtained, they can be used as the basis for a coordinated, international counterdrug initiative, whereby the top twenty consuming countries contribute 10 percent of their annual counterdrug budget into a special World Bank development fund for drug cultivating countries. Those producing countries that agree to eliminate drug production under verification by the UNODC will receive access to the World Bank fund—under the condition that disbursements are earmarked for development programs in areas where cultivation and production is being abolished—and more flexible terms from the International Monetary Fund (IMF).

To complement this program and spur legitimate agricultural exports, the Commission further recommends that participant countries receive improved mid-term trade deals with the United States, Canada, Europe, and Asia. Taken together, these policies levy responsibility for drug eradication on both producing and consuming countries; offer incentives in the form of concrete financial incentives to supplier countries; and—by multilateralizing the fight against illegal drugs—ease the polarizing effect of the current American approach.

2. *Craft a Regional Assistance Strategy by International Donors.* The potential benefit of a regional approach to governance and development assistance in the Andes is often overlooked by donor organizations and countries—especially the United States—in favor of more manageable bilateral relationships. This dynamic is a disincentive to the establishment of common priorities on assistance, consistent standards, and systematized cooperation among international actors in the region.[49] The Commission therefore recommends that the United States, the World Bank, the IMF, the Andean Finance Corporation (Corporación Andina de Fomento, or CAF), relevant UN agencies, regional development banks, and European partners cooperate to develop a regional strategy to harmonize policies, priorities, and funding for governance and development issues, including those related to the rural development trust funds.[50] This strategy could potentially be coordinated under the auspices of the Comunidad Andina, or another existing regional institution. Models to emulate include the joint strategies recently crafted by the U.S. government and the IFIs for a common program and shared responsibilities on money laundering and terrorist finance and the joint European Commission/World Bank Office on Southeast Europe, which acts as a clearinghouse for donor countries and governments by coordinating projects, providing needs assessments, crafting strategies for regional development, and mobilizing donor support.

---

[49]Indeed, the World Bank does not organize the Andean countries into the same administrative scheme. Instead, it groups Colombia with Mexico and apart from Bolivia, Ecuador, Peru, and Venezuela.

[50]See Recommendation 4 in Land Reform and Rural Development, the second section of this report.

3. *Create an Interagency Team to Develop and Implement Targeted Financial Sanctions against Paramilitaries, Guerrillas, and Their Associates and Underwriters.* The U.S. Treasury's Office of Foreign Assets Control (OFAC) is currently leading efforts, in close cooperation with allies, to apply U.S. economic sanctions against narcotraffickers and terrorist organizations. These activities could be intensified through a greater integration and focus of U.S. intelligence and law enforcement agencies and expanded to target the financial supporters of paramilitaries and guerrilla groups.

Using the authorities in the U.S. Patriot Act and under the International Emergencies Economic Powers Act (IEEPA), the administration could create an interagency team with the goal of decapitating these illegal groups financially, by developing strategies to freeze the assets of any persons found to support them monetarily. Mechanisms already exist for this approach, which were used effectively in Serbia against Sloboban Milosevic and were previously employed against particular businesses controlled by members of the Medellín and Cali cartels. The Commission recommends that the United States broaden the list of targets to include paramilitaries and guerrilla groups and seize the bank accounts of those financially involved with those organizations—if necessary, by using the powers provided under the U.S. Patriot Act to take funds out of U.S. correspondent accounts of foreign financial institutions that do business with the prohibited parties in other countries and by requiring the foreign financial institutions to then deduct those funds back in their home countries. International cooperation and consultation is vital to success in this initiative. This approach could create profound disincentives for doing business with those involved in civil conflict and, over time, substantially impair their capacity to fight.

4. *Prioritize Breaking Up the Financial Infrastructure of Drug Cartels by Targeting Money Laundering and Other Syndicates in the United States and Abroad.* A recent four-year Drug Enforcement Administration (DEA) initiative, "Operation

Double Trouble," resulted in the break-up of a major Colombian drug trafficking and money laundering syndicate, from its principal leader to its lower-level money brokers. The investigation was responsible for the seizure of 353 kilograms of cocaine and 21 kilograms of heroin; the arrest of fifty-five drug traffickers and money brokers; and exposure of the cartel's $30 million money laundering racket that used a black market peso exchange, the principal system used in the Western Hemisphere to convert drug money. The international, interagency mission—led by the DEA and assisted by agents from the U.S. Internal Revenue Service, the U.S. Department of Justice, state and local law enforcement agencies, and Colombia's Department of Security—is an excellent example of the benefits of targeting the transnational, high-value end of the narcotics industry. Indeed, Operation Double Trouble reinforces the notion that the black market and money laundering syndicates supply the "oxygen" on which the cartels depend to survive.[51]

The decapitation of the Medellín and Cali cartels in the early 1990s fractured the narcotics industry into diffuse entities and made no appreciable impact on the net export of narcotics from South America. Subsequently, not enough energy and resources have been used to destroy the myriad cartels and syndicates that now operate with ease.

The Commission therefore recommends that, in the immediate term—and as a complement to the multilateralization of counterdrug activities described above—the United States shift significant resources toward the creation and implementation of a high-profile, targeted campaign aimed at cartels' financial underpinnings to combat the existing drug cartels and their laundering syndicates throughout the Andes and the hemisphere. A model for this activity is the array of recent Bush administration initiatives aimed at rupturing the financial assets of terrorist groups such as al-Qaeda. To this end, the Commission endorses a recommendation by the UN Development Programme's *National Human Development*

[51]Eric Green, *U.S. DEA Breaks Up Key Colombian Drug, Money-Laundering Syndicate*, State Department Washington File, U.S. Information Agency, September 9, 2003.

Report 2003 for *Colombia*, which calls on the governments of Colombia and the United States to strike a "new deal" on fighting cocaine and, in particular, to dedicate significantly more resources to fighting traffickers and their associates than currently allocated.[52]

5. *Make Andean Trade Promotion and the Drug Eradication Act (ATPDEA) Permanent until the Advent of the Free Trade Area of the Americas (FTAA) or the Andean Free Trade Agreement (AFTA).* The renewal and expansion of the Andean Trade Preference Act (ATPA) into the ATPDEA was an important step in reinforcing U.S. commitments to economic development in the Andes. However, its temporary nature—the ATPDEA expires in 2006—acts as a disincentive to foreign investment, creating the realistic fear that capital costs invested up front will not be recuperated later in profits if the special preferences granted to Andean countries are withdrawn. The United States is already pursuing full-scale liberalization with the Andean countries in the FTAA. Making the ATPDEA permanent until the passage of the FTAA would create stronger incentives for domestic and foreign investors to allocate their capital to employment-generating export industries. Beginning to address the individual grievances of Andean countries with respect to ATPDEA—Ecuador's desire to export canned tuna is an example—would provide an additional signal of U.S. commitment to development in the region.

6. *Encourage Brazil's "Outward" Foreign Policy on Security, Drugs, and Trade.* Brazil is the world's ninth largest economy and South America's emerging political heavyweight. The government of Luiz Inacio "Lula" da Silva is increasingly exercising political leadership in the Andes and, although a continuation of this policy is expected, much more can be done. As it is doing on trade (in a somewhat different fashion), Brazil could play the role of a South American interlocutor with

---

[52]To read the report in Spanish, see http://indh.pnud.org.co/informe2003_.plx?pga=CO3tablaContenido&f=1072886820&lang=EN.

the international community, lobbying for increased engagement on pressing issues in the Andes related to security, counterdrug policy, economic development, land reform, and democracy consolidation.

Brazil's security is increasingly under threat from growing drug demand and narcotrafficker and gang violence emanating from its neighbor, Colombia. The narcotics industry's spread to Brazil—on both the supply and demand side—has shaken the country, as the scourge of drug-fueled gang violence and corruption infiltrates society and government at all levels. An unstable Brazil would make addressing the Andean crisis immeasurably more difficult, not to mention the seriousness of such a threat to that nation. Brazil's national interests increasingly dictate that it play an active role in addressing the grave security challenges of the Andes and direct international attention and resources to the region. It is a two-way process: the United States and the international community can also take advantage of Brazil's capabilities and interests in the Andes to engage more constructively and cooperatively in the region.

Brazil's capacity for assisting regional security is incipient but improving, with new troops on its northern border and a standing offer, entertained but not yet accepted by Colombia, to provide intelligence from its System for the Vigilance of the Amazon (SIVAM). Enabled by SIVAM with better intelligence to track drug flights that pass through its airspace, Brazil announced it will track incoming aircraft and confiscate illegal cargo when the planes land at their destinations. The new plan does not authorize aerial interdiction (the shooting down of aircraft) that the United States and Colombia practice. Effectively, it signals Brazil's increased attention to the issue without a major shift in policy.[53] Brazil is also participating in other diplomatic initiatives, such as offering to host UN talks with the FARC—a trend that the Commission encourages.

---

[53]Raymond Colitt, "Brazil Targets Colombia Drug Flights," *Financial Times*, October 31, 2003.

THE HUMANITARIAN CRISIS OF REFUGEES
AND THE INTERNALLY DISPLACED

7. *Adequately Fund the UN Humanitarian Action Plan.* Refugees and internally displaced persons present a humanitarian and security challenge of significant magnitude for the region. Estimates vary on the scale of the crisis: in its *Refugees by the Numbers* assessment of 2003, the UN High Commissioner for Refugees (UNHCR) put the number of IDPs in Colombia at 950,000, but other figures have ranged as high as 2.9 million people in a population of approximately 42 million.[54] The number of Colombian refugees has been estimated at over 100,000.[55] Many refugees and IDPs from and in Colombia are noncombatant participants in the irregular violence between armed groups; often they are forced to join the armed groups under the threat of violence.

It is in the humanitarian and national security interests of the Colombian government, the United States, the Andean countries, Panama, Brazil, and the international community to dedicate greater resources to address Colombia's growing humanitarian crisis. The Commission therefore commends the launch, in 2002, of the UN's consolidated inter-agency Humanitarian Action Plan (HAP), a strategy document that increases the humanitarian response capacity of the UN system in Colombia and provides an institutional mechanism for raising funds from the donor community. The HAP currently functions as a complement to the efforts of the government of Colombia. Expanding the HAP's mandate to include alleviation of the incipient humanitarian crises along border areas with the Andean community nations, Brazil, and Panama would complement the UNHCR's regional approach and is

---

[54]See *Refugees by the Numbers 2003*, UN High Commissioner for Refugees, available at www.unhcr.ch; and Gimena Sánchez-Garzoli, *No Refuge: Colombia's IDP Protection Vacuum*, Brookings-SAIS Project on Internal Displacement, available at www.refugeesinternational.org/cgi-bin/ri/bulletin?bc=00593.

[55]*Colombia's Humanitarian Crisis*, International Crisis Group, July 9, 2003, available at www.crisisweb.org.

urgently needed in light of the increasing vulnerability of those populations.[56]

To enable the expansion of the HAP mandate, it is imperative that the donor community increase its funding. Increased funding is also required to guarantee the continuation and amplification of UNHCR's other activities in the region and to support Colombian government institutions concerned with refugee issues.[57] These monies could be raised through current or new bilateral or multilateral donors. Specifically, the Commission calls upon foreign donors (excluding the United States, which already has commited to donate 52 percent of the budget of the HAP) to double their current contributions.[58]

Apart from its contribution to the HAP budget, the U.S. response to the refugee and IDP issue in Colombia includes a $173 million IDP assistance program, run by the U.S. Agency for International Development (USAID) and active until 2005. The Commission encourages a continuation of this level of funding after 2005, until the scale of the crisis diminishes.

IMPROVE SECURITY ASSISTANCE

8. *Amplify U.S. Military Training in Colombia.* Some Colombians would like the U.S. government and its military to make a deeper, more decisive, and more direct strategic investment to end the Colombian conflict—a role the American public and Congress consistently resist. Nevertheless, while it is important to stress that only the Colombians can resolve their

---

[56]Ibid.

[57]See the fourth section of this report, Regional Approaches to Regional Problems, for more detail on Colombia's response to its refugee and IDP crisis.

[58]According to the International Crisis Group, the projected budget of the HAP is $62 million, of which 10 percent has been raised. Principal contributors include the United States (52 percent), Japan (25 percent), Switzerland (5 percent), and Norway (4 percent). Outside the framework of the HAP, the European Commission is the principal contributor to Colombia for humanitarian issues, spending $8.6 million in 2002.

conflict, the United States can provide more training without tempting comparisons to an interminable quagmire.

Under the aegis of Plan Colombia, only 400 U.S. military service members and 400 U.S. private military contractors are permitted in Colombia at any one time to conduct counterterrorism, counterinsurgency, and counterdrug work. This cap is intended, at least in part, to preserve congressional support for U.S. action in Colombia by preventing a "slippery slope" of increasing U.S. involvement and keeping ownership of Colombian security primarily in Colombian hands. Although the reasons for the cap are valid, the current cap limits merit reexamination.

At present, the Colombian ombudsman's office reports that human rights violations are almost nonexistent among the Colombian counterdrug, infrastructure protection, and counterterrorism battalions vetted and trained by the United States.[59] Raising the current cap on the number of military and contract personnel able to conduct training would accelerate the professionalization of the Colombian armed forces. Such a proposal would require congressional review and approval. Similarly, revising the current fixed ratio of military-to-civilian personnel to a more flexible distribution would give the commander of the U.S. Southern Command (South Com) greater discretion in directing the use of military and contract resources.

9. *Continue to Prioritize Progress on Human Rights for Security Assistance.* Respect for human rights is at the core of U.S. counterterrorism and counterdrug training policy in Colombia. Bipartisan support for U.S. policy toward Colombia depends on continued adherence to the vetting of Colombian soldiers who receive U.S. military training; the embedding of human rights education into the military training curriculum; and the use of human rights certification of Colombian military and police units in accordance with the Leahy amend-

---

[59]Andes 2020 Commission interview, Office of the Ombudsman, Government of Colombia, Bogotá, May 12, 2003.

ment law.[60] Amplifying the vetting, training, and certification process of Colombian military and police units will give the United States more scope for ensuring that positive changes in the security environment do not come at the expense of human rights. Further internalization of respect for human rights within Colombia's military will be contingent upon its termination of ties with the United Self-Defense Forces of Colombia (AUC) and other paramilitary groups; it is therefore important that the United States does not shy away from addressing this issue when disbursing aid and in its training and vetting activities.[61]

Respecting human rights is not solely an American responsibility. In recognition of the findings by the U.S. Department of State's *Country Reports on Human Rights Practices (2002)*—specifically, that "tacit arrangements between local military commanders and paramilitary groups in some regions" exist where "members of the security forces actively collaborated with members of paramilitary groups"—the Commission calls upon the government of Colombia to increase funding to the ombudsman and inspector general's office to investigate and expose these "tacit arrangements"; immediately suspend officers against whom there is credible evidence of collusion with paramilitary groups; and pursue investigations, and where necessary prosecutions, against senior military officers who have been accused of links to paramilitary groups.[62] The Commis-

---

[60]The so-called Leahy amendment, sponsored by Senator Patrick Leahy (D-VI, the ranking Democrat on the Foreign Operations Subcommittee of the Senate Committee on Appropriations), requires the U.S. secretary of state to certify progress by the Colombian military in respecting the human rights of the civilian population and severing ties with the paramilitary groups as a condition to disburse U.S. funds. Furthermore, with the approval of the secretary of state, the amendment empowers the U.S. ambassador to terminate funding for specific units of the Colombian armed forces who are not certified as meeting human rights standards.

[61]It is, of course, important that similar standards are adhered to by other countries involved in bilateral security assistance to Colombia, such as the United Kingdom.

[62]*Country Reports on Human Rights Practices (2002)*, U.S. Department of State Bureau of Democracy, Human Rights, and Labor, March 31, 2003, available at www.state.gov/g/drl/rls/hrrpt/2002/18325.htm.

sion also endorses a March 2003 report from the UN High Commissioner for Human Rights (UNHCHR) office in Colombia, which enumerates twenty-seven recommendations for improving Colombia's human rights record; calls upon the Colombian government to implement the report's policy recommendations; and encourages the UN, the U.S. State Department, and human rights nongovernmental organizations (NGOs) to monitor and publicly comment on the implementation process.[63]

Finally, the Commission recommends that the Alvaro Uribe administration commission an independent panel of international jurists and other experts to assess the government's progress in breaking ties with paramilitaries, with a secondary focus on the matter of paramilitarism and illegal armed groups in Colombia. Analogous to similar commissions in Peru and Chile on truth and reconciliation and in Central America on paramilitaries, the independent commission would have plenary power to carry out its investigation as an autonomous body, and would issue a report to the Colombian public and the international community.

10. *Coordinate U.S. Counterterrorism Policy in Colombia.* To gain visibility for the region's security crisis and effectively coordinate U.S. security policy in Colombia and the region, the Commission recommends the assignment of a flag officer, at

---

[63]Notable recommendations from the UNHCHR report include establishment, by the attorney general, of a task force to investigate possible links between members of the armed forces and the paramilitary groups; introduction, by Congress, of a judicial order to restrict the powers of the armed forces to prosecute military justice cases; and collaboration between the vice president, the minister of defense, minister of the interior, and public ombudsman to make effective the "system of early alert" for preventing rights abuses to communities at risk. Overall, the recommendations target specific Colombian institutions and pertain to six areas: prevention of abuses and protection of human rights; the internal armed conflict (aimed at the illegal armed actors and armed forces); the rule of law and impunity; economic and social rights; the promotion of a culture of human rights; and increased assistance and technical cooperation between the UNHCHR office and relevant Colombian government institutions. Marta Luciz Ramirez, at that time the defense minister of Colombia, disputed the accuracy of the UN report, citing Defense Ministry statistics with contrasting findings; see "MinDefensa Presentaron informe oficial de derechos humanos 2002–2003," *El Tiempo*, September 10, 2003.

the level of brigadier general, to the U.S. embassy in Bogotá. This officer would head the office of defense cooperation in Colombia under the ambassador but would have a regional portfolio and also report to the commander of South Com. His responsibilities would include coordinating U.S. security activities throughout Colombia and the Andes, monitoring security developments in the region, and maintaining a line of communication between the U.S. ambassadors in the region and the South Com commander.

11. *Offer a Senior U.S. Defense Review Team to the Colombian Defense Ministry.* In order to analyze where improvements can be made for the entire apparatus of the Colombian defense ministry and armed forces, the Commission recommends offering a U.S. defense review team, comprised of senior military officials from a cross-section of the armed forces, to develop the Colombian equivalent of the 1968 Goldwater-Nichols Defense Organization Act. Appropriate areas for review and recommendation include civilian control of the armed forces; armed forces command relationships with the national police; relations between and across the services; and the military education system, with particular focus on human rights issues, laws of land warfare, and rules of engagement. Depending on the outcome of the Colombia experience, analogous teams can be offered to defense ministries around the region, according to their requests.

Beyond the review process, it would be constructive for the U.S. senior defense team, in coordination with the country team, to begin a dialogue with their Colombian counterparts regarding peace negotiations with the FARC and the National Liberation Army (ELN). Preparation of an overarching strategy for the political end game—and specifically the military's role in that scenario—is long overdue, as it is clear that the Colombian policy elite has not fully considered the political and security dimensions of any ultimate outcome involving the reintegration of guerillas into the national fabric.

The U.S. senior defense review team could also perform a useful function in the regional context by convening multinational consultations with counterpart officers and civilian defense officials in Colombia, Venezuela, Ecuador, Peru, Bolivia, Panama, and Brazil, as a supplement to ongoing bilateral consultations. These multilateral gatherings would focus on crafting a common security doctrine to jointly address regional transnational threats.

12. *Stop Penalizing Countries for Failure to Issue Article 98 Exemptions.* In 2003, the George W. Bush administration suspended millions of dollars in aid to Ecuador and Colombia for failure to issue an "Article 98" exemption to Americans in-country under the International Criminal Court (ICC) treaty. Such action works at cross-purposes with the objective to create stability on the region's borders—as, for example, in Ecuador, where the armed forces are critical to border security to the north and have taken steps to strengthen cross-border cooperation. The administration's action essentially deprives the United States of precisely the leverage and cooperative disposition it desires. It also sends the message that—despite its own extraordinary efforts to protect U.S. sovereignty from possible ICC-related encroachments—Ecuadoran public opinion on sovereignty-related matters is of little concern.

Colombia, meanwhile, lost $5 million in 2003 due to sanctions related to Article 98. Rather than risk losing $130 million in 2004, Colombia agreed to the exemption—a step that Colombian and international human rights groups suggest may deprive Colombia of the possibility of referring to the ICC for prosecution those paramilitary or rebel leaders charged with violating international humanitarian law.

13. *Use Available U.S. Government Tools to Fight Corruption in the Andes.* Corruption is pervasive in the Andes, but the U.S. government does have tools to combat its corrosive influence where U.S. interests are affected.[64] The U.S. Foreign Corrupt Practices Act is a tool already in place to fight corruption, but its scope is necessarily restricted. Similarly, although

---

[64]See section four of this report, Regional Approaches to Regional Problems, for anti-corruption recommendations targeted to the Andean governments.

the United States's Millennium Challenge Account (MCA) prioritizes corruption control in determining aid recipients—making it a potentially useful tool in rooting out corruption—it is initially limited to countries eligible for assistance from the International Development Association (IDA). Currently, Bolivia is the only Andean country eligible for MCA funds.[65] However, a positive development in the fight against corruption is a new multiagency task force convened under the powers of the U.S. Patriot Act, which is targeting financial assets laundered into the United States by foreign leaders suspected of public corruption. The Commission recommends that the task force—currently a pilot operation involving the departments of Homeland Security, State, Justice, and the Treasury—be institutionalized, and its methods and means of information-sharing be systematized and coordinated with the anti–money laundering work of the Drug Enforcement Administration. Expanding the task force's capacity to include an outreach program, through which members of the public can anonymously report offenders, also merits consideration.

14. *Ratify and Monitor Implementation of the Inter-American Convention against Illicit Manufacturing of and Trafficking in Firearms, Ammunitions, Explosives, and Other Related Materials (CIFTA).* Rampant black market trading of small arms, gas, precursor chemicals for drugs, and other materials represents a grave threat to peace and security in the Andean region. The CIFTA convention is regarded as a model set of norms for stemming black market flows of arms, but there remains a significant gap between theory and practice.[66] The Commission endorses the CIFTA convention, established in 1997, and calls

---

[65]Eligibility for MCA funding is projected to increase annually. In fiscal year (FY) 2004, only countries that can borrow from the IDA and that have per capita incomes below $1,435 are eligible. In FY2005, all countries with per capita incomes below $1,435 will be considered, regardless of IDA status; and by FY2006, all countries with incomes up to $2,975—including Colombia, Ecuador, and Peru—will be eligible. See www.mca.gov.

[66]For example, although Nicaragua ratified CIFTA in 1999, in 2001, Nicaraguan police and military authorities sold 3,000 used AK-47 assault rifles to a middleman posing as a broker for the Panamanian police, who then delivered the shipment of weapons to Turbo, Colombia, into the hands of the AUC.

upon the U.S. Senate to ratify it immediately.[67] Ratification of CIFTA by the United States—the largest producer of arms in the world—will greatly enhance its credibility.

Beyond ratification of CIFTA, a credible U.S. commitment would be signaled by the creation of an interagency task force to monitor and interdict arms sales entering the Andes from Central America and elsewhere via the black market.[68] Like the new U.S. multiagency task force now investigating money laundering in Latin America, this initiative would be crucial in bridging the current gap between rhetoric and reality with respect to arms trafficking. The Commission further recommends that a portion of U.S. aid from the Andean Counterdrug Initiative be earmarked to support the strategy and capacity-building initiative—called the "Andean Plan for the Prevention, Combat, and Eradication of Illicit Trafficking of Small and Light Arms"—launched in March 2003 by the Andean Community Foreign Ministers. On a parallel track, it is important that the United States and the European Union continue to adequately fund and implement the UN's "Programme of Action to Prevent, Combat and Eradicate the Illicit Trade in Small Arms and Light Weapons."

---

[67]CIFTA was submitted to the Senate in 1998.

[68]The main sources of arms in the Andes are still small-scale black market routes, not "bulk purchases." Because most of the arms come from external sources, the FARC and the AUC are struggling for control of the best land and sea smuggling routes. Kim Cragin and Bruce Hoffman, *Arms Trafficking and Colombia*, RAND Corporation for the Defense Intelligence Agency, November 2003.

REGIONAL APPROACHES TO
REGIONAL PROBLEMS

Many of the strategic, political, economic, development, social, humanitarian, and security challenges faced by individual Andean states are mirrored in the other countries of the region. However, the United States, the international community, and, indeed, the Andean governments themselves, have done little in the way of developing integrated, cross-border approaches to common problems. Yet ignoring the regional scope and impact of the problems in the Andes hobbles attempts to remedy them. Thus, just as the Commission recommends the multilateralization of international efforts in the Andes where possible, so it advocates greater cooperation, communication, and collaboration among the Andean countries themselves. Regional problems with regional impact require regional approaches.

Although security is by no means the only area that requires a regional strategy, it is perhaps the most urgent and it is the obvious starting point. As explained in the first section of this report, Findings, the Andean states do not command effective sovereignty over their territory. In other words, they are incapable of patrolling their entire territory with police or armed forces; providing the rule of law throughout the country; fostering democratic access to markets and economic security; and policing the movement of people and goods across borders. As a result, security threats—whether terrorist, transnational, or common criminal in nature—reinforce and exacerbate profound governability challenges throughout the region and beyond.

Although every Andean state is susceptible to common security deficiencies, Colombia's security challenges are clearly unique. Colombia is the only government that confronts three illegal armed groups, plus a multitude of proxy militias that protect the interests of "baby" drug cartels.[69] Precisely because the Colombian government is unable to fight its various enemies in every corner of the country, the illegal armed groups can operate throughout huge tracts of ungoverned territory, much of which is located in the broad regions bordering Panama, Venezuela, Ecuador, and Brazil.

Although the borders that Colombia shares with its five neighbors total 6,004 kilometers—twice the length of the border shared by the United States with Mexico—the other Andean countries have, until recently, refused to acknowledge that they are inextricably connected to Colombia and to each other. At the same time, it is essential to recognize that historically—and regardless of the ideology of Colombia's neighboring governments—informal ties have existed as much with the illegitimate forces in Colombia as with legitimate government forces. The long-established modus vivendi between the civilian and military authorities—particularly in Venezuela and Ecuador—with the Revolutionary Armed Forces of Colombia (FARC), the National Liberation Army (ELN), paramilitaries, and drug traffickers has yet to be offset by sustained government-to-government operational and institutional ties.

Ecuador and Venezuela, although not the only parties implicated in this behavior, are good examples. The harsh ideological tone of the Hugo Chávez government, on the one hand, and the weakness and historic neutrality of the Ecuadoran government, on the other, weaken the legal authority and security environment on the borders and do nothing to undermine the capacity of illegitimate forces and supporting industries that already violate their respective sovereignties. For all of the above reasons, therefore, it is not surprising—though nonetheless disquieting—that there is little in the way of an integrated approach to security in the Andes.

---

[69]Although gathering statistics on the number of illegal armed actors in Colombia is an inexact science, it is estimated that, in aggregate, the illegal armed groups, paramilitaries, and private militias of the eighty-two drug cartels constitute 50,000 combatants. The Colombian armed forces regularly deploy approximately 40,000 troops in its theater of operations, out of a total of 55,000 combat-ready soldiers. As of November 2003, the combined manpower of the Colombian armed forces is 125,000. The Uribe administration envisions increasing this figure to 225,000 soldiers by the end of 2006.

Colombia's neighbors complain bitterly of bearing the lion's share of responsibility for securing their borders with Colombia. They also argue that Plan Colombia, with its emphasis on counterdrug and security assistance to Colombia, gives nominal consideration to the regional consequences of its policies. It is true that Colombian security forces focus on weakening the FARC and protecting infrastructure and do not play a large role in patrolling frontiers or combating illegal armed groups in the border regions.[70] But while Colombia and its neighbors trade diplomatic blows over the polemics of individual cases of weapons trades between armed forces and illegal groups, denial of responsibility by parties on all sides is becoming patently untenable, as the security situation takes on a bona fide regional character.

Security is not the only area that is conducive to regional action: trade, economic development, anticorruption efforts, and humanitarian action to ease the refugee crisis stemming from Colombia's conflict can also be effectively addressed on a regional basis. The following recommendations include strategies to leverage regional capabilities and strengths in pursuit of collective and national interests. On the other hand, there are some issues that are common across the Andes—such as the low level of state revenues from tax and the problems of tax collection and enforcement—but that cannot be tackled in a regional framework. In these cases, where common problems exist but a cross-border approach is unviable, the Commission's recommendations focus on actions that individual states can take but that are, in principle, applicable to all of the Andean countries.

1. *Deepen Domestic Revenues.* State revenue-generating systems in the Andes are underperforming. Revenue inflows from income and property taxes, value-added taxes (VAT) on goods and services, and direct royalty flows from commodities

---

[70]With the notable exception of border cooperation between Ecuador and Peru since 1998 (in the aftermath of conflict between the two state armed forces), the security forces in the region have not as yet crafted mechanisms for coordination in border patrol, intelligence sharing, or other tactical ground, air, and river operations. The Commission notes that Colombia has recently committed to sending approximately 400 soldiers to its border with Venezuela, which is already manned by 12,000 Venezuelan troops.

such as oil are inadequate in relation to the amount that could be generated from the domestic economy, were it not for widespread tax evasion, loopholes, and weak government enforcement.[71] This underperformance is symptomatic of the institutional weakness prevalent in the Andes and is a reason why governments do not make sufficient investments in the overall development of the nation—on issues ranging from social spending to funding security forces, public works, and local governance. Internally, revenue-generating systems in the Andes suffer from an extremely narrow tax base, rampant evasion and corruption, and a regressive tax structure characterized by a dependence on VAT. Externally, pressure from the international community, in particular from the International Monetary Fund (IMF), to maintain budget austerity and controlled spending does not call sufficient attention to the extremely important limiting factor on the other side of the equation: low government revenue.

The Commission argues that equitable reform of state revenue systems will require more than a revision of tax codes. Lasting reform will necessitate a broad effort to generate greater civic responsibility, inform all citizens about the taxes they do and do not pay through a public education campaign, and improve the quality and fairness of the internal revenue collection regime. Improving the state's revenue capacity in a broad-based way would enhance institution building and democratic consolidation, above and beyond the tangible benefits of increased spending capacity.

Reform of the revenue-generating systems could begin with a public campaign by Andean governments to seriously crackdown on tax evasion through the elimination of loopholes and increased enforcement, with penalties for nonpayment. Collection and enforcement of property tax is particularly crucial.[72] Furthermore, with the exception of Bolivia, Andean governments

---

[71]Nancy Birdsall and Auguso de la Torre, *Washington Contentious: Economic Policies for Social Equity in Latin America,* Carnegie Endowment for International Peace and Inter-American Dialogue, 2001.

[72]See section two in this report, Land Reform and Rural Development, for a specific recommendation on property tax reform and penalties for nonpayment.

are middle-income nations and are developed enough to revise their dependence on VAT—a cash cow of the state but a levy that burdens the poor as much as the rich.[73]

Taxes can also be expanded on luxury items, corporate income, and tourism, in addition to an overall increase in levies on the top 10 percent of income earners in the Andes— who pay comparatively a much lower rate than their counterparts in the United States—without creating negative incentives for investment and growth. By broadening their tax bases through a lower minimum rate of income required for contribution and a more progressive structure, Andean governments could induce greater revenues.

2. *Make Tax Revenues a Part of IMF Discussions.* The Commission recommends that the U.S. executive director at the IMF encourage staff to study and report on the options for countries to expand their effective tax revenue collections from higher-income households, via administrative, enforcement, and, if appropriate, policy changes; and urges that the progressive nature of tax systems (including the mix of property, personal, corporate income, capital gains, VAT, and other taxes) be systematically assessed and reviewed in the context of IMF Article IV reports and lending proposals. The U.S. Treasury could also take other appropriate steps to encourage the IMF and other international financial institutions (IFIs) to address revenue issues, especially problems such as evasion, exemption, and loopholes that reduce the taxes paid by higher-income persons.

3. *Negotiate an Andean Free Trade Area (AFTA).* The Commission supports U.S. efforts to work toward the creation of a Free Trade Area of the Americas (FTAA). Long-term goals, however, need not prevent the United States and its Andean partners from launching efforts to harness the power of free trade to promote economic growth in the near term. An Andean Free Trade Area, pursued on a parallel track with the

---

[73]Nancy Birdsall and Augusto de la Torre, *Washington Contentious: Economic Policies for Social Equity in Latin America*, Carnegie Endowment for International Peace and Inter-America Dialogue, 2001.

FTAA, is a critical first step toward greater integration and offers the greatest promise for harnessing trade for real development benefits in the region. In November 2003, at the Miami ministerial meeting of trade representatives of the Americas, the United States formally announced it would pursue bilateral trade agreements with, first, the governments of Peru and Colombia, and, second, with Bolivia and Ecuador. The Commission views this regional approach as a positive development that can encourage intraregional economic and political integration toward the broader goal of AFTA.

Although efforts to implement a Central American Free Trade Agreement (CAFTA) provide a model for AFTA, new ground can be broken in ensuring that market liberalization—which promises development gains for the Andes—does not come at the expense of the poorest segments of the population. To that end, it is critical that all five Andean countries begin by lowering tariff barriers intraregionally to one common level, in the form of a customs union; and that, in negotiating trade deals, the United States fund social safety nets to supply an economic safeguard for those citizens in developing nations who are negatively affected by the short-term effects of liberalization.[74]

4. *Aggressively Combat Corruption, Especially in the Extractive Industries.* Exacerbated by the drug trade, entrenched corruption throughout the Andes and Latin America impedes economic growth and undermines the rule of law. For example, it is estimated that diversions from state budgets in Colombia alone amount to $1.76 billion per year (or close to two points of gross domestic product, or GDP, per capita). An estimated half of all state contracts in that country involves payoffs, at an annual cost of $480 million to the economy; $5 billion per year is laundered; and putting an end to corruption would enable Colombia to reduce its public fiscal deficit by 80 percent.[75]

---

[74]In the technical recommendations section of this report, the Commission outlines in greater detail the need for social safety nets and other measures to mitigate the short-term effects of trade liberalization on developing countries' poor sectors. See Appendix A, Recommendation 1.

[75]"Muchos Discuros, Pocos Goles," *El Tiempo*, August 26, 2003.

A crucial tool in fighting corruption is improving tax collection and enforcement. Another step the Andean governments can take is to create new, or strengthen existing, anticorruption ministries, ensuring their autonomy and giving them authority commensurate with an ombudsman's office.[76] It is also necessary that the ministries' remit includes punitive powers against both payers and recipients of bribes, in the latter case focusing primarily on corporate, as well as individual, participants.

In Colombia, the national government has taken steps to usurp the power of some local authorities in oil-rich regions involved in payments to the ELN and other rent seekers. The Commission applauds this action and regards it as a model, when initiated legally, for other governments in the region.

The extractive industry is under particular pressure from some governments and nongovernmental organizations (NGOs) to take a stand against corruption by increasing transparency and accountability in dealings with host governments. The G-8's Extractive Industries Transparency Initiative, spearheaded by the United Kingdom, is developing a model for publishing the payments that extractive companies make to governments and those governments' revenues. The Commission supports the G-8 initiative and emphasizes the importance of applying the standards of transparency and accountability equally to publicly traded, privately owned firms; government-owned oil companies, such as PDVSA in Venezuela; and host governments themselves. The Commission also endorses the United Nations (UN) Development Programmme's Commission on the Private Sector and Development and recommends that it lend its moral authority to encouraging the energy industry—and the private sector as a whole—to commit to global good citizenship and best practices.

---

[76]In 2003, the head of Colombia's anticorruption initiative resigned because he felt his work was being ignored by other government officials. See "Muchos Discuros, Pocos Goles," *El Tiempo*, August 26, 2003.

5. *Take Greater Action on the Refugee and Internally Displaced Persons (IDP) Crisis.*[77] The Colombian government's response to its refugee and IDP crisis has, thus far, been largely ad hoc, uncoordinated, and underfunded.[78] Accordingly, the Commission recommends that the government of Colombia create action and accountability on the issue through the establishment of a special adviser to the president for humanitarian affairs, and solicit aid from donor governments and institutions specifically for that office. The special adviser would be responsible for strengthening cooperation between the central government and the nineteen state institutions that comprise the National System of Integral Assistance to the Population Displaced by Violence (SNAIPD). Other priorities of the special adviser and his or her staff would include collaboration with the UN High Commissioner for Refugees (UNHCR) offices in Bogotá, Quito, and Caracas, and with other international humanitarian agencies, NGOs, the Andean Community, neighboring governments, and the Organization of American States (OAS); oversight of the allocation of department budget funds for IDP assistance and for safe return to their original or new homes; ensuring that all registered IDPs receive public assistance as stipulated in Law 387 of the Colombian Constitution; and coordination with international donors on food security, basic rural housing, victims of violence compensation, and educational and health programs.

Cooperation on refugee issues can foster positive bilateral and regional relationships among Colombia and its neighbors. The Commission encourages the neighbors to continue facilitating the return of displaced Colombians through the new bilateral "Mechanisms for dealing with the phenomenon of displacement," and to demonstrate a commitment to this issue by

---

[77]See also the third section in this report, U.S. and International Community Engagement, for a recommendation concerning the international response to Colombia's humanitarian crisis.

[78]Although the Uribe administration reported resettling 7,218 displaced families in 2002, over half of new internally displaced persons received no government assistance. Many were not even registered with Colombia's Social Solidarity Network (RSS), the administrative entity responsible for coordinating assistance.

addressing it at the next meeting of the Andean Community of nations. [79] It is also vital that the Andean countries fully cooperate with the regional UNHCR offices to establish clear standards for assessing refugee status and receiving asylum seekers; combat xenophobia and racial discrimination; and provide basic health care and other essential services to these vulnerable groups.

6. *Create an AmeriPol and AmeriJust to Combat Transnational Crime.* The European Union (EU) has created Europol, a regional institution to carry out exchange of law enforcement information on a continent-wide basis, to facilitate prosecutions of criminals whose activities cross borders by creating a base in which the police agencies in Europe can place liaison officers and create joint operations. There is currently no institution in the Americas to facilitate cross-border law enforcement intelligence and strategies and carry out operations against criminals in more than one country. An AmeriPol could fill that critical gap, providing greater law enforcement intelligence capacity and operational support to all law enforcement agencies operating in the Americas. Initially, an AmeriPol could be financed by the United States alone, or by the United States, Canada, and Mexico. Alternatively, it could be financed by a formula based on the relative size of the populations, or economies, of the participating countries.

The creation of an AmeriJust for a similar sharing of strategies by prosecutors also merits consideration. This institution would be comparable to an existing EU body, EuroJust, which improves common prosecutorial capacity against serious cross-border or transnational crime.

7. *Update the Inter-American Treaty of Reciprocal Assistance (the Rio Treaty).* The 1947 Inter-American Treaty of Reciprocal Assistance (the Rio Treaty) remains the hemisphere's formal defense mechanism. The Rio Treaty calls for members of the OAS to respond collectively to aggression against any

---

[79] Colombian Foreign Ministry communiqué to the staff of the Andes 2020 Commission, July–August 2003.

member state, although it does not oblige members to fulfill any specific duty to commit troops or arms. In light of the post–Cold War, post–September 11 geopolitical realities—although recognizing the tradition of Latin American nation-states to uphold the principle of noninterference in the sovereign affairs of others—it is appropriate for the OAS to review and update the collective security doctrine of the hemisphere. Such a review will allow the OAS to better address the myriad asymmetrical threats of drug trafficking, terrorism, crime, and humanitarian crises faced by its member states. The OAS Special Conference on Security, held in Mexico City in October 2003, articulated an updated convergence of principles and methods for realizing peace and justice in the hemisphere but did not update the Rio Treaty. This is an unfortunate development, as the issue deserves to be studied further and pushed up the agenda. Building on the condemnation of terrorism expressed by all OAS members at the signing of the Inter-American Convention against Terrorism in 2002, the Commission further recommends that the OAS Special Committee on Security study the possibility of creating a standby multinational peacekeeping capacity for the Americas, under OAS auspices, that would focus on humanitarian and security crises resulting from natural disasters and civil conflict. This peacekeeping capacity force, although training together as the new NATO rapid response force does, would essentially be reserve commitments from nations to be called upon by the OAS Permanent Council when a crisis occurs.[80]

8. *Move against the FARC, the United Self-Defense Forces of Colombia (AUC), and the ELN.* All five Andean community nations ratified the OAS Inter-American Convention against Terrorism, promulgated in June 2002. In keeping with the standards of the Convention, the Commission recom-

---

[80]"Perspectives on the Americas on Military Interventions, Conference Summary," *Regional Responses to Internal War, Number Three*, Fund for Peace, June 2002; Colonel Joseph R. Nuñez, *A 21st Century Security Architecture for the Americas: Multilateral Cooperation, Liberal Peace, and Soft Power*, Strategic Studies Institute, July 2002.

mends that the Andean countries, plus Brazil and Panama, adopt and implement legislation to cooperate on border control; prevent and interrupt terrorist financing and activities; and otherwise treat the FARC, the ELN, and the AUC as terrorist groups until they enter into humanitarian and ceasefire accords and halt criminal activities.[81]

9. *Increase the Frequency of Binational Commission and Neighborhood Commission Meetings of Colombia with Andean Community Members, plus Panama and Brazil.* Through concerted effort on the part of the Uribe administration and neighboring governments, an incipient dialogue on border security issues is underway through the mediums of binational border commissions (Colombia, with Ecuador and Panama, respectively); neighborhood commissions (Colombia, with Peru and Brazil); and presidential negotiating commissions (Colombia and Venezuela). On a periodic basis, these binational working groups—which typically involve representatives of the Defense, Justice, and Foreign Ministries, and are part of the annual presidential summits—discuss and coordinate joint security mechanisms to combat the movement of illegal groups, share intelligence, and address the issues related to displaced Colombian citizens in border zones. Except in the case of Venezuela— with which Colombia has had a presidential negotiating commission since 1990—the commissions were formed very recently: with Panama and Ecuador in 2002, and with Brazil and Peru in 2001.[82] Not surprisingly, therefore, the border commissions are still developing institutional capacity. The Commission recommends that the United States support these initiatives by encouraging its Andean partners to increase the frequency and quality of border commission meetings and by offering to send observer missions if desired. U.S. Southern Command (South Com) representatives could also be offered as facilitators for the meetings.

---

[81]*Colombia and Its Neighbors: The Tentacles of Instability,* International Crisis Group, April 8, 2003.
[82]Ibid.

10. *Continue and Enhance Security Cooperation between Colombia and Venezuela.* Security cooperation between Venezuela and Colombia, which share an active, 1,274-mile-long border, has improved since the presidential summit between Presidents Alvaro Uribe and Hugo Chávez in April 2003. Venezuela currently deploys two brigades of troops (12,000 soldiers) along the border with Colombia. In August 2003, meanwhile, Colombia dispatched an army battalion (consisting of 400 troops) to its eastern border for the first time, in recognition that Venezuelans are increasingly victims of kidnapping and violence by Colombia's armed groups. Nevertheless, cooperation between the two countries remains insufficient. It is therefore vital that joint security cooperation between the two nations is enhanced, especially since Colombia is using the Venezuelan border as a test case for troop deployment to other active frontier regions. U.S. South Com engagement with both militaries could take advantage of this opportunity for joint security operations against illegal armed groups, and could potentially foster the beginning of a genuine "combined operational ethic" between the two armed forces.

Other priorities for the Colombians and Venezuelans—with technical assistance from the United States, if necessary—include real-time intelligence sharing between the militaries and border police; the articulation of a well-defined, cooperative operational response to prevent illegal armed groups from obtaining sanctuary across the border in Venezuela; and negotiation of an agreement allowing Colombian and Venezuelan militaries to employ "hot pursuit" tactics, whereby an active military unit can pursue its target across the border.

Although the heightened potential for violence along the Colombia-Venezuela border makes it an immediate priority, the Commission recommends that similar cooperation mechanisms eventually be employed along Colombia's other borders.

11. *Fuse and Strengthen the OAS Drugs, Crime, and Arms Programs.* The Commission recognizes the importance of the OAS Multilateral Evaluation Mechanism (MEM), which operates under the Inter-American Drug Abuse Control Commis-

sion (CICAD) and provides a forum for coordination and cooperation through regular evaluations of progress against drugs.
Amplifying the mandate of the MEM and the Inter-American Convention against Illicit Manufacturing of and Trafficking
in Firearms, Ammunitions, Explosives, and Other Related Materials (CIFTA) to produce a regular "Accessories to Transnational Crime Report" would spotlight the business enterprises
and individuals operating as brokers in the informal economy
to move illegal commerce. The initial goal of the report would
be to publicly shame such enterprises and individuals and
provide fodder to the relevant law enforcement agencies for investigation and prosecution.

ADDITIONAL AND DISSENTING VIEWS

Full and permanent access of the Andean countries to the U.S. market is a central recommendation of the Commission. Ideally, the report would make clear that an Andean Free Trade Agreement should be shaped so as to be consistent with a future agreement negotiated in the World Trade Organization's Doha round, including without additional obligations (for example with respect to capital markets) on the Andean members. In addition, the recommendation (in Appendix A) to strengthen criteria for Andean Trade Promotion and Drug Eradication Act eligibility (presumably until and unless a treaty is agreed upon), should not be "conditional" on performance in the manner proposed for the large aid transfers planned under the proposed Millennium Challenge Account. Although appropriate for aid transfers, in the case of access to U.S. markets, such conditionality and accompanying periodic "evaluations" create uncertainty for potential local and foreign investors and undermine the hope that secure access would enhance growth, development, and security in the Andean region by encouraging a more dynamic and competitive private sector. For example, in the area of labor standards, instead of conditionality, emphasis in the interagency process of the United States could be on the Andean countries' cooperation with a reporting role for the International Labor Organization (ILO), with maximum transparency within countries on ILO reports on labor conditions.

Nancy Birdsall
Endorsed by Anthony Stephen Harrington

Certainly, Andean countries, and especially Colombia, the principal focus of this report, are plagued by deep social and economic ills. Colombia in particular needs help. Although many of the Commission's numerous recommendations deserve strong endorsement (e.g., measures to strengthen the Justice Department), others are more questionable (e.g., detailed rural reform proposals without greater analysis of their impact). And some recommendations seem misguided because they are based on the premise that Colombia can overcome its multiple problems without first making major progress in suppressing violent groups that profit from widespread intimidation and narcotrafficking. Rather than criticize current U.S. foreign policy, the report should explain that, while Colombia has many needs, citizen security—carried out with a vigorous respect for human needs and rights—is key to preserving the country's democracy and improving the lot of its people.

Ian Davis

The report correctly points out that for more than two decades, U.S. Andean policy has been driven by faith that drug eradication overseas will solve America's drug problems. Although this supply-side approach has been proven wrong time and again, faith in eradication still prevails, for example, in shaping much of the administration's multi-billion-dollar commitment to Plan Colombia. It should by now be clear that even if the Colombians succeeded in eradicating most of their drug crops—which is highly unlikely even with intensive aerial spraying—Americans would have little trouble finding drugs. As long as millions of consumers are willing to pay for drugs, there will be no shortage of suppliers. If one source is interrupted, others quickly fill the gap. The report concludes that the United States has become "extremely effective at eradicating coca by country," but it does not take into account that any such "success" is short-lived and more than offset by rising production in other countries in the region. Bolivia, which cut coca production by half between 1998 and 2001 at great political cost, has resumed widespread cultivation. (U.S.-assisted eradication in Bolivia was a key factor in the recent populist uprising that forced President Gonzalez Sanchez de Lozada to resign.)

With the infusion of major U.S. military aid and eradication support, Colombia has cut coca production by 15 percent. Yet since the inception of Plan Colombia, net coca cultivation in the Andean region has increased. Meanwhile, cocaine (and Colombian heroin) coming into the United States from the Andes is cheaper and more potent than ever.

Better solutions to U.S. drug problems will be found not in other countries but in reducing the demand for drugs here at home. Treatment is far less expensive than the alternatives. A 1994 RAND study found that $34 million invested in treatment reduced cocaine use as much as $783 million spent for foreign source country programs or $366 million for interdiction. Nonetheless, this administration continues to spend more than two-thirds of the nearly $20 billion annual drug control budget on supply control efforts—eradication, interdiction, and law enforcement. Prevention and treatment receive less than one-third of the total—about $5.5 billion. For two decades, under both Democratic and Republican administrations, America's drug war has concentrated on reducing supplies, not demand.

This year, however, the federal drug budget looks different. As the report notes, spending for supply and demand appear to have been brought into balance. But nothing really has changed. The new budget is deceptive: it does not reflect new priorities but simply reorganizes the way expenditures are reported. The Office on National Drug Control Policy has removed almost $8 billion from the drug budget that is devoted to prosecuting and incarcerating drug offenders. In fact, this spending is likely to increase in the coming years. The public should not be lulled into believing that U.S. policy has finally recognized the primary importance of reducing America's appetite for drugs. Our national drug policy closes its eyes to the reality of what works; prevention and treatment remain severely underfunded, while the United States continues to spend billions for eradication programs abroad.

Mathea Falco
Endorsed by Anthony Stephen Harrington,
H. Allen Holmes, and James D. Zirin

The Commission's report takes a holistic view of Andean policy issues, and those of Colombia in particular. I support this approach as the only one likely to generate an integrated and useful menu of policy recommendations that cuts across necessary political, economic, and social domains, and does so regionally. The report is notable for drilling down on issues creatively and generating a substantive body of recommendations. I do not share in all of these and perhaps even less some of the introductory findings. For example, I remain troubled that the report voices a tired line of the past regarding the possibility of "divisive commitment of U.S. military... resources," a red herring heard for years among Latin American and U.S. critics of a leadership role for the United States in the region. On the whole, however, I find the report's conclusions timely building blocs for bipartisan policy initiatives.

The major preoccupation with the report lies with the sequencing of the recommendations. Land reform and rural development deserve the attention the report gives to these issues; however, I remain unconvinced that launching major initiatives in these areas will bear much of an early harvest without a robust resolution of Colombia's internal insurgency. I begin with the premise that the security of Colombia's democratic government is nonnegotiable, but the report devotes only seven lines of its recommendations directly to dealing with insurgency and paramilitary groups. By implication, this assigns to the report's social and economic reform recommendations a significant role in helping to decisively defeat this violence. I do not believe, however, that the Revolutionary Armed Forces of Colombia and the National Liberation Army will respond positively merely to such social and economic reforms. Moreover, the highly politicized nature of land issues, and a possibly heavy-handed intrusion from the international community in these matters, could in the short run reinforce skepticism among conflict-weary Colombian stakeholders.

George A. Folsom

I regret that the report makes a series of ad hominem assertions and counterproductive recommendations that mar the end result. I also fear that, because of its overwhelming focus on Colombia, the report may underestimate or misunderstand the challenges that could arise from political developments in Venezuela. I do, however, commend the report for alerting readers to the magnitude of the difficulties faced by the Andean region. Moreover, I endorse the report's emphasis on the desirability of (a) greater regional and multinational cooperation in addressing both the supply and demand components of the drug problem, (b) a comprehensive and coordinated U.S. strategy toward the Andean region that goes well beyond drug eradication and interdiction efforts in Colombia, (c) implementation of the Free Trade Area of the Americas and reduction of barriers to trade among the Andean countries and with the United States and Europe, and (d) enhancement (in many cases creation) of state presence (in security, health, education, etc.) in rural sectors, and provision of effective access to property rights and market mechanisms to the most disenfranchised in the region.

Sergio J. Galvis

The report identifies the magnitude and complexity of the problems with which the countries of the Andean region are grappling, and many of its recommendations make good sense. Other recommendations are not as carefully thought out. Despite its call for regional approaches to key issues, the paper concentrates overwhelmingly on Colombia and treats Venezuela and Ecuador more as afterthoughts.

I applaud the report's urgent call for an "aggressive, comprehensive regional strategy from the United States, the international community, and local actors ... a strategy that goes beyond drugs to channel resources to far-reaching rural and border development and judicial and security reform, and that will mobilize the commitment and capital of local elites, as well as U.S. and other international resources." I endorse the report's focus on a regional approach supported by a well-coordinated, multilateral effort involving all the countries of the region and Brazil, as well as traditional donors.

Particularly important, in my view, is the emphasis on the need for "diffusion of political and economic power in each country in an accountable and democratic fashion" coupled with strengthening the presence of the state throughout the countries' national territories, including by providing effective judicial, education, health, as well as security services, to all areas. The report's call for energetic measures to increase rural incomes is right on target, although I harbor no illusions about how difficult this will be to achieve in many areas and caution against overreliance on land reform per se. By definition, such an effort will require creative "alternative development" schemes.

Measures to ensure the Andean countries' broad access to the markets of the United States, Europe, and other more developed countries are absolutely vital and, therefore, I object to suggestions that trade privileges be conditioned beyond the commitments undertaken by the negotiating parties in an Andean Free Trade Agreement with the United States, a hemispheric Free Trade Area of the Americas, the World Trade Organization's Doha round, or individual bilateral free trade agreements. Such conditionality would, in effect, discriminate against the Andean countries, creating disincentives for essential investment and reforms.

Finally, I have no doubt that the Andean region's security issues, including those generated by narcotics, which are most acute in Colombia, must be addressed aggressively and merit the sustained involvement of all Colombia's neighbors and friends. Yet I am concerned that some of the report's security recommendations seem to imply an increased "Americanization" of the battle against the illegal armed groups. In my view, that would over time undermine the credibility and effectiveness of the local forces who, in the final analysis, will determine the outcome of this truly arduous struggle.

Alexander F. Watson
Endorsed by Jonathan Winer

COMMISSION MEMBERS

NANCY BIRDSALL* is the Founding President of the Center for Global Development. Prior to launching the center, Birdsall served for three years as Senior Associate and Director of the Economic Reform Project at the Carnegie Endowment for International Peace. From 1993 to 1998, she was Executive Vice-President of the Inter-American Development Bank. Before joining the Inter-American Development Bank, she spent fourteen years in research, policy, and management positions at the World Bank, most recently as Director of the Policy Research Department.

DANIEL W. CHRISTMAN, Co-Chair of the Andes 2020 Preventive Action Commission, is the Senior Vice President for International Affairs at the United States Chamber of Commerce in Washington, D.C. Previously, he was the President and Executive Director of the Kimsey Foundation. Before heading the Kimsey Foundation, Lieutenant General Christman (U.S. Army, Ret.) served for five years as the Superintendent of the United States Military Academy at West Point. Prior to that assignment, he served two years as Assistant to the Chairman of the Joint Chiefs of Staff in the Pentagon, where he traveled with and advised President Bill Clinton's Secretary of State on a broad range of military and national security issues. During the Gulf War in 1991, he headed a strategic planning group that advised the Army's Chief of Staff on war prosecution policies. He also served in President Gerald Ford's administration as a member of Henry Kissinger's National Security Council staff.

NELSON W. CUNNINGHAM is Managing Partner of Kissinger McLarty Associates. He was Special Adviser to President

---

Note: Commission members participate in their individual and not institutional capacity.

*The individual has endorsed the report and submitted an additional or dissenting view.

Bill Clinton for Latin American affairs and served as Chief of Staff at the White House to President Clinton's Special Envoy for the Americas, Thomas F. "Mack" McLarty III. He has served as a lawyer at the White House, and was General Counsel of the Senate Judiciary Committee. He previously served in the Justice Department as a federal prosecutor in New York, specializing in international financial investigations and prosecutions.

IAN DAVIS* is the Vice President for International Affairs at Occidental International Corporation, the government affairs subsidiary of Occidental Petroleum Corporation. Prior to joining Occidental, he was the Director of International Government Relations at Fluor Corporation, a global construction and engineering firm. He is also a member of the State Department's Advisory Committee on International Economic Policy, where he currently chairs a subcommittee on public-private partnerships and public diplomacy.

MATHEA FALCO* is the President of Drug Strategies, a nonprofit research institute, and was Assistant Secretary of State for International Narcotics from 1977 to 1981.

GEORGE A. FOLSOM* is the President and CEO of the International Republican Institute (IRI), a nonprofit organization that monitors elections and helps political parties, civil society, and governments build democracy in more than fifty countries. Prior to joining IRI, he advised global investment banks and corporations on the impact in the financial markets of U.S. trade, national security, and foreign policies as a Principal in the Scowcroft Group. Folsom has extensive experience in government, serving in the Ronald Reagan and George H.W. Bush administrations, as well as in the private sector.

SERGIO J. GALVIS* directs Sullivan & Cromwell's Latin America practice, which comprises approximately fifty-five lawyers who have significant experience in the region. During his eighteen years at Sullivan & Cromwell, he has counseled Latin American businesses and governments, as well as international financial institutions and companies, in connection with some of the most significant transactions in the region. He is also a Director and General Counsel of the Council of the Americas and a member of the Council on Foreign Relations.

ANTHONY STEPHEN HARRINGTON* is President of Stonebridge International, LLC, an international strategic advisory firm based in Washington, D.C., co-founded with former National Security Adviser Samuel R. Berger. Previously, he served as U.S. ambassador to Brazil. He was previously Chairman of the President's Intelligence Oversight Board, Vice Chairman of the President's Foreign Intelligence Advisory Board, and a member of the congressionally created Commission on the Roles and Capabilities of the U.S. Intelligence Community.

JOHN G. HEIMANN, Co-Chair of the Andes 2020 Preventive Action Commission, was Chairman of the Financial Institutions Group of Merrill Lynch and a member of its Executive Committee until his retirement in 1999. He is a member of the Group of Thirty. Mr. Heimann is the Senior Advisor to the Financial Stability Institute of the Bank for International Settlements, of which he was the Founding Chairman. He was the U.S. Comptroller of the Currency, Commissioner for the New York State Division of Housing and Community Renewal, and Superintendent of Banks for the State of New York. He is a Member of the Advisory Committee of the Toronto International Leadership Center for Financial Sector Supervision, and also belongs to the Citizens Committee for New York City, New York City Housing Partnership. He has been a Member of the Board of the Federal National Mortgage Association and the Federal Deposit Insurance Corporation, and was Chairman of the Federal Financial Institutions Council. He was voted "Housing Man of the Year" by the National Housing Conference in 1976.

---

*The individual has endorsed the report and submitted an additional or dissenting view.

H. ALLEN HOLMES* is a Consultant to Georgetown University. Previously, he was Assistant Secretary for Special Operations and Low Intensity Conflict at the U.S. Department of Defense. Before that post, he had a long career in the Department of State, including positions as the Ambassador-at-Large for Burden Sharing, the Director of the Bureau for Political-Military Affairs, and the U.S. ambassador to Portugal.

ROBERT C. ORR is the Executive Director for Research at the Belfer Center for Science and International Affairs at the John F. Kennedy School of Government at Harvard University. Previously, he was Vice President of the Council on Foreign Relations and Director of its office in Washington, D.C.

MARK SCHNEIDER is the Senior Vice President of the International Crisis Group (ICG), the Program Director for the ICG's new Latin America program, and head of its Washington office. Previously, he served as Director of the Peace Corps. He has held senior positions at the U.S. Agency for International Development and at the Pan American Health Organization, a regional office of the World Health Organization.

BARBARA SHAILOR is the Director of the International Department of the AFL-CIO. She oversees the work of the American Center for International Labor Solidarity, working through twenty-six field offices to support unions in fifty-five countries in Africa, the Americas, Asia, and Europe. She also serves as a senior adviser to AFL-CIO President John Sweeney on foreign and international policy issues. Prior to joining the AFL-CIO, she directed the International Department at the International Association of Machinist and Aerospace Workers.

GEORGE SOROS is President and Chairman of Soros Fund Management LLC, a private investment management firm that serves as principal adviser to the Quantum Group of Funds, a series of international investment vehicles. He is also Chairman of the Open Society Institute and the founder of a network of philanthropic organizations that are active in more than fifty countries. In 1992, he founded the Central European University, with its primary campus in Budapest. His latest book is *George Soros on Globalization.*

JULIA E. SWEIG is Senior Fellow and Deputy Director of the Latin America Program at the Council on Foreign Relations. Her latest book, *Inside the Cuban Revolution: Fidel Castro and the Urban Underground,* was published in June 2002 and won the 2003 American Historical Association's Herbert Feis Award, given to the best book of the year by an independent scholar.

ARTURO VALENZUELA is Professor of Government and Director of the Center for Latin American Studies in the Edmund A. Walsh School of Foreign Service at Georgetown University. Prior to joining the Georgetown faculty, he was Professor of Political Science and Director of the Council of Latin American Studies at Duke University. During the Bill Clinton administration, Valenzuela served as Special Assistant to the President and Senior Director for Inter-American Affairs at the National Security Council and, prior to that position, as Deputy Assistant Secretary for Inter-American Affairs in the Department of State.

ALEXANDER F. WATSON* is Managing Director of Hills & Company, an international consulting firm. From 1996 until 2002, he was the Vice President of the Nature Conservancy. Prior to joining the Conservancy, he was a career Foreign Service Officer for more than thirty years, serving in his last assignment as Assistant Secretary of State for Inter-American Affairs from 1993 to 1996. He was Ambassador to Peru from 1986 to 1989, and was also the Deputy Permanent Representative to the United Nations and the Deputy Chief of Mission in Brasília, Brazil; Bogotá, Colombia; and La Paz, Bolivia.

CHARLES WILHELM is Vice President and Director of the Homeland Security Office at the Battelle Corporation. He recently retired from the Marine Corps as a four-star general. In his final military assignment, he served as Commander of the U.S. Southern Command, where he was responsible for all U.S. military activities with the thirty-two nations of the Caribbean and Central and South America. Wilhelm was a career infantry officer and a veteran of combat operations in Vietnam, Lebanon, the Persian Gulf, and Somalia.

JONATHAN WINER* is an attorney at Alston & Bird LLP in Washington, D.C. He was previously the U.S. Deputy Assistant Secretary of State for International Law Enforcement. Prior to that, he was Chief Counsel and principal Legislative Assistant to Senator John Kerry (D-MA). He also served on the Council on Foreign Relations's Task Force on Terrorist Financing.

JAMES D. ZIRIN* is a Partner in the New York office of Sidley Austin Brown & Wood LLP, which he joined in 1993 and where he is a member of the litigation department. He was previously a partner at Breed, Abbott & Morgan. For three years, he was an Assistant U.S. Attorney for the Southern District of New York, serving in the criminal division under Robert M. Morgenthau.

COMMISSION OBSERVERS

FULTON ARMSTRONG has been the National Intelligence Officer for Latin America since June 2000. Previously, he served as Chief of Staff of the Directorate of Central Intelligence Crime and Narcotics Center; two terms as a Director for Inter-American Affairs at the National Security Council (1995–97 and 1998–99); and as Deputy National Intelligence Officer for Latin America (1997–98). Before that, he held various analytical and policy positions, including one as the political-economic officer at the U.S. Interests Section in Havana.

ALBERTO IBARGÜEN is Publisher of the *Miami Herald*. Previously, he was Executive Vice President of *Newsday*. He served in the Peace Corps in Venezuela, was the Peace Corps Program Director in Colombia, and went on to practice law in Connecticut. Mr. Ibargüen is Vice Chairman of the Public Broadcasting System. He also sits on the boards of the Freedom Forum, the Inter-American Press Association, and the Committee to Protect Journalists.

EDWARD JARDINE is the President of Procter & Gamble in Venezuela and the Andean region. He has been with Procter & Gamble in Venezuela since 1978. He is also a member of the Board of Directors–President Investment Committee of the Venezuelan American Chamber of Commerce.

JAMES LEMOYNE is the Special Adviser on Colombia to the United Nations Secretary-General. Previously, he was a senior foreign correspondent and foreign policy analyst, specializing in conflicts and peace processes in Latin America, the Middle East, Africa, and Europe.

CARL MEACHAM advises the Chairman of the Senate Foreign Relations Committee, Senator Richard Lugar (R-IN), on policy regarding the Western Hemisphere. Prior to working for the

Committee, he was senior adviser for foreign relations and energy issues to Senator Charles Schumer (D-NY). Before that, he was a Legislative Assistant for Senator Harry Reid (D-NV). Previously, he served as Special Assistant to the Deputy Secretary of Commerce, Robert L. Mallett.

WILLIAM L. NASH is the John W. Vessey Senior Fellow and Director of the Center for Preventive Action at the Council on Foreign Relations.

JANICE O'CONNELL is a Professional Staff Member of the U.S. Senate Foreign Relations Committee and is Senior Foreign Policy Assistant to Senator Christopher J. Dodd (D-CT).

ROGELIO PARDO-MAURER is the Deputy Assistant Secretary for Western Hemisphere Affairs at the U.S. Department of Defense. Before joining the Department of Defense, he was President of Emerging Market Access, a consulting firm based in Washington, D.C. He has also been a Managing Partner of Access NAFTA Project Management and President of Chartwell Information Group. He has worked as a specialist in Latin American and U.S.-Hispanic issues at the American Enterprise Institute and the Center for Strategic and International Studies.

LINDA ROBINSON is a Senior Writer on Latin America at *U.S. News and World Report*. She has also been a Senior Editor at *Foreign Affairs* and an Assistant Editor at *The Wilson Quarterly*.

THOMAS SHANNON is the Senior Director for Western Hemisphere Affairs at the National Security Council. Prior to this appointment, he was the Deputy Assistant Secretary in the Bureau of Western Hemisphere Affairs at the Department of State. His other State Department posts have included the Director of Andean Affairs (2001–2002), U.S. Deputy Permanent Representative to the Organization of American States (2000–2001), Director for Inter-American Affairs at the National Security Council (1999–2000), and Political Counselor at the U.S. Embassy in Caracas, Venezuela (1996–99).

APPENDIXES

APPENDIX A:
ADDITIONAL TECHNICAL RECOMMENDATIONS

ECONOMIC DEVELOPMENT AND TRADE

1. *Incorporate Protections for Subsistence Farmers and Workers.* Minimizing the inevitable shocks that follow opening markets requires targeted protection for the most vulnerable populations: subsistence farmers and workers. The terms of agricultural liberalization in the Andean Free Trade Agreement (AFTA) can best protect rural farmers and prevent potentially destabilizing shocks and dislocation by phasing out tariffs on staple crops only gradually—giving subsistence farmers time to adapt—while increasing access to the U.S. market for cash crops more quickly. To protect workers, the benefits of AFTA can be made conditional on progress in labor law reform and implementation, country by country and sector by sector. As in the U.S.-Cambodia free trade agreement, the International Labor Organization (ILO), working with the office of the U.S. Trade Representative (USTR), can be given a vital reporting role in determining whether Andean countries have complied with international labor standards.

Since free trade also imposes social costs—as sectors adjust to competition from lower-priced, competitive goods produced abroad—trade capacity building strategies can also recognize the need for adjustment assistance and investment in social protection programs to minimize the negative short-term impacts of liberalization. Just as the wealthy countries of Europe assisted Portugal and Greece with their transition from agricultural to modern economies, the United States can support Andean nations in developing social safety nets, particularly targeted at sectors likely to experience displacement as a consequence of liberalization. Technical assistance is already available through the ILO and the United Nations's

Economic Commission on Latin America and the Caribbean (ECLAC), but financial resources will have to come from the Andean countries' wealthier trading partners, such as the United States.[83]

2. *Renew U.S. Membership in the International Coffee Organization (ICO).* The global coffee crisis is severely damaging producers in Colombia and the Andes. According to the World Bank, coffee prices in real economic terms are less than one-third of their 1960 level and considerably below the cost of production for the majority of coffee farmers. These conditions cause spikes in unemployment and the dislocation of growers in the rural regions of Colombia, leading farmers to cultivate illegal, but highly profitable, crops such as coca and poppy. This trend is damaging U.S. geopolitical interests in Colombia, as unemployed coffee growers are sucked into narcotrafficking and are more susceptible to joining illegal armed groups. As an example of the economic loss suffered by Andean coffee-producing nations, Colombia alone has suffered a nearly 50 percent decline in coffee revenue over the past decade, undermining a crucial revenue source for fighting poverty and bolstering security.

Because it is the world's largest coffee consumer and the principal international strategic actor in the Andes, it is in the national economic and geopolitical interest of the United States to help revive the coffee industry by rejoining the International Coffee Organization. The ICO is the principal intergovernmental organization for strengthening ties between coffee farmers and purchasing companies, as well as producing and consuming nations. It serves as a forum and advocacy group, promoting consumption and lobbying for a sustainable coffee economy—chiefly through recommendations to reconcile the problems of the global bean glut and inadequate returns for coffee producers on their sales.

---

[83]A report from the Carnegie Endowment for International Peace, *NAFTA's Promise and Reality: Lessons from Mexico for the Hemisphere*, 2003, contains similar recommendations and insights regarding the short-term challenges faced by developing nations during the initial stages of trade liberalization.

Since the United States resigned its ICO membership in 1993, the organization has ended its support for a quota-based model that set baseline prices for trading coffee beans; it now advocates market-based solutions. The National Coffee Association—which represents the spectrum of U.S. coffee industry enterprises—promotes U.S. membership, and six leading representatives of the House International Relations Committee—including Chairman Henry Hyde (R-IL) and Ranking Member Tom Lantos (D-CA)—argued for the United States to rejoin the body immediately in a letter to Secretary of State Colin Powell dated September 8, 2003. Indeed, U.S. membership in the ICO would be a positive development for American consumers. Membership in the ICO would allow the United States to use its influence on behalf of high-quality coffee growing countries such as Colombia, helping them discover profitable markets and supplemental income through alternative cash crops. Furthermore, effective U.S. leadership at the ICO would lead to improved economic conditions in the rural sectors of the Andes and curtail the ominous trend of Andean farmers cultivating illegal crops and entering into partnerships with illegal armed groups. Chairman Hyde has promised $500,000 to finance the return of the United States to the ICO; the fee for membership is lower than the chairman's funding proposal. The Commission endorses Chairman Hyde's letter and encourages the Bush administration to respond positively by earmarking funds from the Andean Counterdrug Initiative (ACI) to rejoin the ICO.

3. *Strengthen the Criteria, and Systematize the Process, for Determining Country or Sectoral Eligibility for Benefits of the Andean Trade Promotion and Drug Eradication Act (ATPDEA).* The ATPDEA already spells out a wide range of eligibility criteria, which, if properly enforced, would act as an incentive for domestic policy reform by Andean countries. But the interagency process responsible for determining country eligibility, led by the USTR, has not stringently applied these criteria, as evidenced by the continued violations of workers' rights in the Ecuadoran banana industry. The performance-based

approach introduced in the president's new Millennium Challenge Account (MCA)—in which determinations of assistance levels are conditioned on transparent and public indicators of governmental performance—provides a more appropriate model for determining qualification. The office of the USTR can set in place a rigorous process for evaluating whether countries meet eligibility criteria, setting out clear indicators—such as intellectual property rights and industry and government respect for labor rights—that prioritize pro-development policies.

4. *Reform the Overseas Private Investment Corporation (OPIC) to Increase Foreign Direct Investment.* Current statutory constraints restrict OPIC from providing political risk insurance coverage to many projects of substantial potential impact in the Andes and other developing areas. Accordingly, current OPIC investments in the Andean region are limited and focused primarily in the energy sector, rather than in supporting textile manufacturing and other small-scale industries most likely to create jobs. OPIC coverage could be a catalyst for investment in the Andean countries if two key statutory changes were put into effect. First, change the measure of OPIC evaluations of projects from the "U.S. effects" standard now in place to a "U.S. net economic benefits" test. Effectively, this means opening up the OPIC portfolio to encourage investments that will, on balance, have collective benefits for U.S. workers, firms, and communities, rather than staying with the less development-friendly standard, which eliminates from contention any project that costs a single U.S. job. The second change would allow OPIC to provide coverage to foreign-owned firms with a "significant" U.S. presence, defined as employing 250 or more workers.

5. *Support National Trade Capacity Building Strategies.* Rural areas and secondary cities merit a particular focus of U.S. support for trade capacity building. Assistance could target small and medium-sized businesses in each country and focus on providing technical assistance to enable more efficient access to U.S., or local and regional, markets. Matched with participa-

tion by local capital, such efforts will further promote private-sector development and improve the capacity of the Andean countries to compete in the U.S. market. Efforts in this area could be modeled on current U.S. assistance to Central American countries in preparation for the Central American Free Trade Agreement (CAFTA). The Chilean national export promotion agency is also a good model.

6. *Strengthen Financial Systems.* The Andean nations have all experienced severe problems with their banking systems. This has been due, in differing degrees, to economic dislocations caused by external debt renegotiations, poor bank management, questionable credit decisions, cronyism, and, in some cases, corruption. A flawed banking system distorts the allocation of credit, which inevitably causes economic dislocations. In order to strengthen their financial institutions, there has been a trend toward consolidation and permitting foreign bank entry. Likewise, there have been steps to strengthen banking supervision. Nevertheless, much more needs to be done. The Commission recommends that these nations take increased advantage of the programs offered by the International Monetary Fund (IMF), the World Bank, the Financial Stability Institute of the Bank for International Settlements, and the Toronto International Leadership Center for Financial Supervision. All of these programs provide for the education and training of financial supervisors.

7. *Impose a Global Tax.* The imposition of a global tax—under which governments can tax their citizens' income regardless of where it is earned—will also increase government revenues, decrease the potential for corruption, and actively engage wealthy citizens in their country's welfare. Adoption of a global tax may require a tax treaty between the United States and the country in question—an arrangement the United States currently has with over fifty countries, including Venezuela.[84] Because many who avoid tax in their home countries also

---

[84]Although Venezuela has entered into the tax treaty with the United States, it has not yet acted to impose tax on its nonresident citizens.

evade taxation in the United States, it is in the interest of both the Andean countries and the United States to enact and enforce these treaties.

GOVERNANCE AND THE RULE OF LAW

8. *Build Capacity through the Creation of a Regional Justice Center.* In the United States, the Federal Judicial Center has developed a series of initiatives to strengthen the administration of justice throughout the federal judiciary and the state court systems, dealing systematically with such issues as alternative dispute resolution, automation, computers and technology, bankruptcy, case management, court governance and management, criminal law and procedure, discovery and disclosure, evidence, expert witnesses, intellectual property, judicial ethics, long-range planning, mass torts, prisoner litigation, sentencing, speedy trials, and voting rights. The approach undertaken by the Federal Judicial Center domestically could be extended throughout the Americas to provide more systematic and coherent professional development, advice in the nuts and bolts of administration, and assistance in legal drafting and norms of conduct. This institution could potentially be developed under the auspices of existing regional structures, such as the Organization of American States (OAS), the Andean Secretariat, or the Andean Commission of Jurists, to train judges and officers of the court. The international financial institutions, the OAS, and the European Union (EU) are potential sources of funding.

9. *Endorse the New International Law Enforcement Academy (ILEA) in San Jose, Costa Rica.* The United States has established international law enforcement training academies in Budapest, Bangkok, and Botswana and is currently in the process of establishing such an academy for Latin America in San Jose, Costa Rica. ILEA (San Jose) would be the first common institution for the Americas to serve as a training facility for law enforcement officers, promoting inter-American

education, harmonization of standards and norms, sharing of techniques, and personnel networking. The Commission supports the creation of ILEA in Costa Rica, and recommends that its training curriculum focus on the following pressing needs: anticorruption strategies; money laundering; trafficking of people, drugs, and guns; narcotics interdiction; computer crime; counterterrorism strategies and techniques; database management; cross-border information sharing; appropriate technologies (including strategies for computerization in less-affluent countries); security; judicial and regulatory process; and white-collar investigations.

ILEA is jointly managed by the U.S. Departments of State, Justice, and the Treasury, and by the Costa Rican government. In order for ILEA to become a worthwhile regional resource, it is necessary to broaden access so that other countries and relevant institutions—including the OAS's Inter-American Drug Abuse Control Commission (CICAD) and the Caribbean Community and Common Market (Caricom)—can participate in its management, oversight, and, when appropriate, funding. It is also crucial for all trainees to be vetted by the relevant U.S. embassies according to the Leahy amendment standards, and for there to be transparency with regard to the academy's curriculum, course content, students, and instructors.

SECURITY

10. *Enhance Intelligence Sharing.* U.S. advisory teams have been effective in providing the Colombian military with the intelligence information necessary to carry out attacks against the senior leadership of the Revolutionary Armed Forces of Colombia (FARC), the National Liberation Army (ELN), and the United Self-Defense Forces of Colombia (AUC), but the Colombian armed forces have not acted on this intelligence. However, there is still room for improvement in intelligence sharing. The Commission recognizes the limitations of this cooperative effort due to current U.S. personnel cap restrictions, but

recommends that U.S. advisory teams continue, and intensify, intelligence sharing as an incentive for the Colombian armed forces to take aggressive action against the leaderships of the illegal armed groups. The Commission does not endorse American military action on the basis of that intelligence but suggests that the U.S. teams encourage their Colombian counterparts to appropriately follow through on actionable intelligence. On a regional basis, tapping the resources offered by the recently launched Brazilian radar surveillance system would broaden the effectiveness of this critical "ops-intelligence" tactic.

11. *Draw On Pentagon Funding Allocated for Counterterrorism for Regional Security Initiatives.* Under the aegis of the ACI, most security and counternarcotics programs supported by the United States in the Andes are administered by the State Department's Bureau of International Narcotics and Law Enforcement (INL). In the last two years, Congress allocated billions of dollars to the Pentagon for the war on terrorism, and granted the Bush administration the authority to conduct counterinsurgency, counterterrorism, and counterdrug activities in Colombia. The Commission recommends that counterterrorism funds housed in the Department of Defense be made available for the regional security initiatives proposed in this report.

12. *Review the Technology in the Theater.* After a steady flow of U.S. military technology was sent to the theater of operations in Colombia, some critical American aircraft, helicopters, and surveillance platforms were diverted to U.S. missions in Afghanistan and Iraq and have not returned. Although the capacity of the American armed forces is stretched, it is nevertheless necessary that a review of the technology allocated to the theater in Colombia is conducted, in order to maximize Colombian and regional security capacity. In particular, the Commission recommends providing Maritime patrol aircraft (MPA) to monitor the Caribbean and Pacific coasts of Colombia and Ecuador, where large shipments of cocaine are transported by

"fast boats" to delivery vessels. AWACS (airborne warning and control system) aircraft and helicopters are also recommended for use in airspace surveillance and for border security along the Colombia-Venezuela frontier region.

13. *Maintain Military-to-Military Relations with Venezuela.* Despite the poor diplomatic relations between the United States and Venezuela, the Commission recommends maintaining and amplifying military-to-military relations between the two countries. Personnel exchanges, military contacts, and student exchanges at U.S. military schools are almost the only functioning components of the bilateral relationship and can serve as a vehicle for cooperation on counterdrug and other security-related issues—as evidenced by Venezuela's constructive cooperation on counterdrug activities such as poppy eradication and interdiction.

14. *Utilize Brazil's System for the Vigilance of the Amazon (SIVAM).* In recent years, Brazil has fortified its vast border region with Colombia and offered to share intelligence from its SIVAM radar system. This potentially valuable resource for fostering cross-border security is currently underutilized. The Commission commends Brazil's assertive role in engaging the Andean community on regional security challenges and recommends that Colombia move more quickly to work with the Brazilian Defense Ministry on collaborative intelligence gathering regarding illegal cross-border activities. The Commission also recommends the United States facilitate this process by resolving the current interagency dispute over legal authorities required to best take advantage of SIVAM-generated intelligence.

APPENDIX B:
ECONOMIC STATISTICS AND INDICATORS

Andean Economic Growth, 1995–2004

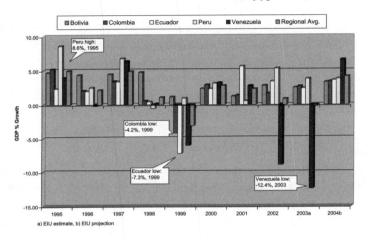

Source: Institute for International Finance, Economist Intelligence Unit (EIU) 2003.

Per Capita GDP Growth, 1995–2002

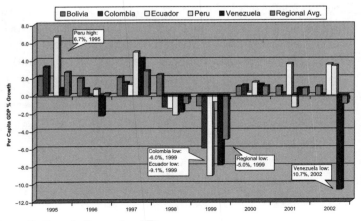

Source: Institute for International Finance, 2003.

Foreign Direct Investment, 1997–2002

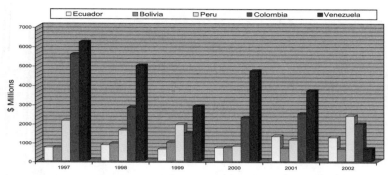

Source: International Financial Statistics, International Monetary Fund (IMF), 2003.

Portfolio Investment Flows, 1997–2002

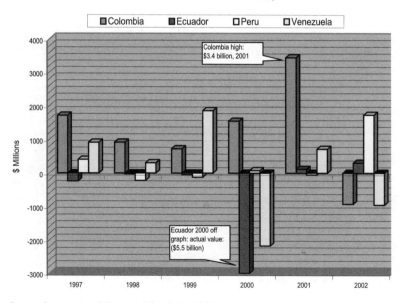

Source: International Financial Statistics, IMF, 2003.

Tax Revenues in Andean Countries, 2002

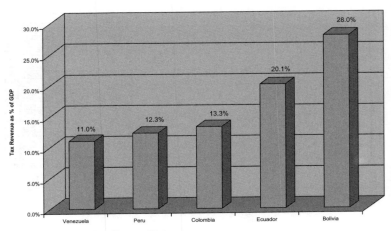

Source: Economist Intelligence Unit, 2003.

Economically Active Population (EAP) and the Informal Sector

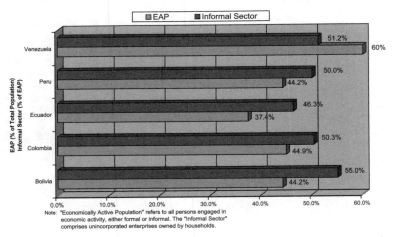

Sources: International Labor Organization, 2002, and Economist Intelligence Unit, 2003.

Andean Unemployment Rates, 1995–2002

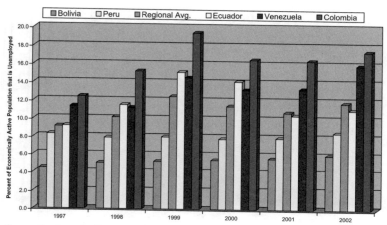

Source: Institute for International Finance, 2003.

Income Inequality

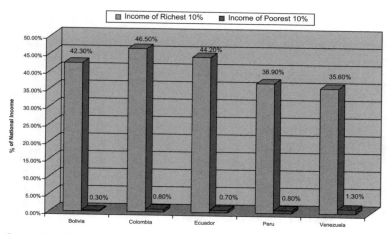

Source: World Bank, Inequality Report, 2003.

Land Tenure Inequity

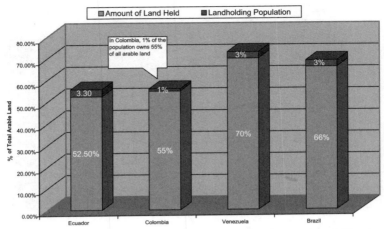

Sources: Ecuador: *Ecuador—An Economic and Social Agenda in the New Millennium,* World Bank, 2003; Colombia: UN Reliefweb Reporting, 2003; Venezuela: Economist Intelligence Unit, 2003.

Poverty

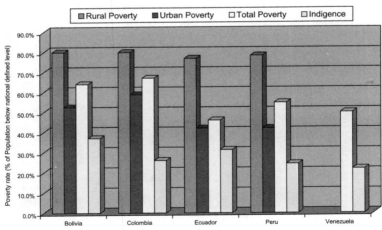

Sources: Government sources, 2003, and UN Economic Commission for Latin America and the Caribbean (ECLAC), 2002.

Compostition of U.S. Assistance to the Region—
"Guns and Butter" 2000–2004
Source: U.S. Department of State.

"Guns and butter" is defined as the breakdown between the funding categories of military/police versus social/economic programs, respectively. There are a multitude of specific initiatives which the U.S. government supports in the Andean region under both of these classifications. A sampling of U.S. programs includes drug interdiction, counterterrorism training, judicial reform, and assistance to citizens displaced by the Colombian conflict.

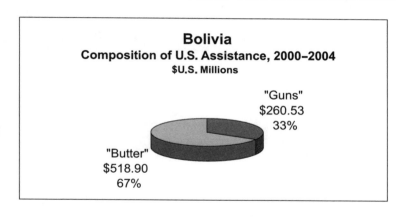

Bolivia
Composition of U.S. Assistance, 2000–2004
$U.S. Millions

"Guns"
$260.53
33%

"Butter"
$518.90
67%

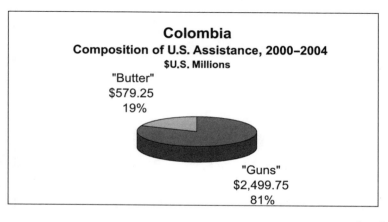

Colombia
Composition of U.S. Assistance, 2000–2004
$U.S. Millions

"Butter"
$579.25
19%

"Guns"
$2,499.75
81%

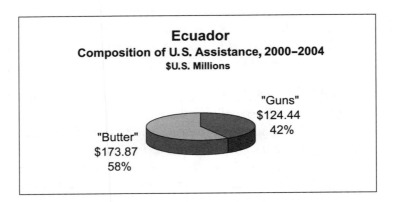

Ecuador
Composition of U.S. Assistance, 2000–2004
$U.S. Millions

"Guns"
$124.44
42%

"Butter"
$173.87
58%

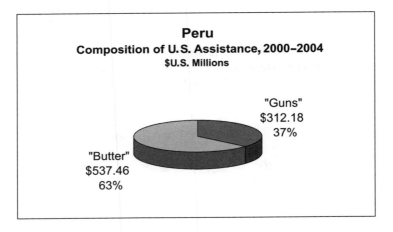

Peru
Composition of U.S. Assistance, 2000–2004
$U.S. Millions

"Guns"
$312.18
37%

"Butter"
$537.46
63%

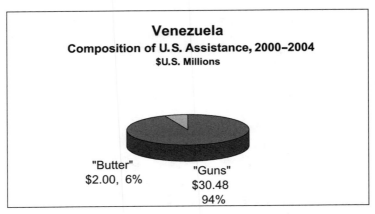

Venezuela
Composition of U.S. Assistance, 2000–2004
$U.S. Millions

"Butter"
$2.00, 6%

"Guns"
$30.48
94%

Percent of Total U.S. Crude Imports

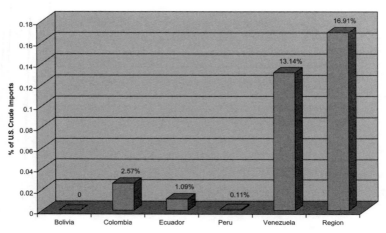

Source: Energy Information Administration, U.S. Dept. of Energy, 2003.

Proven Natural Gas Reserves

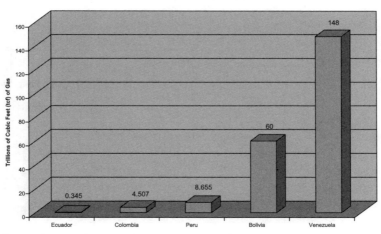

Source: Energy Information Administration, U.S. Dept. of Energy, 2003.

Andes Coca Cultivation

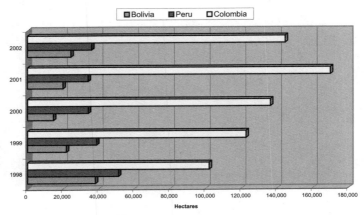

Source: U.S. Department of State, 2003.

Net Coca Cultivation:
Columbia, Peru, and Bolivia

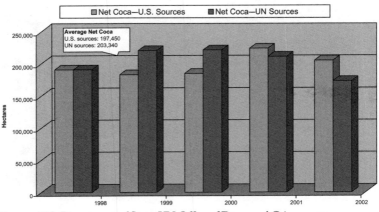

Sources: U.S. Department of State, UN Office of Drugs and Crime, 2003.

APPENDIX C:
ILLEGAL ARMED GROUPS
IN THE REGION

(in alphabetical order)

NATIONAL LIBERATION ARMY (EJÉRCITO DE LIBERACIÓN NACIONAL, OR ELN)—COLOMBIA

Description
Marxist insurgent group formed in 1965 by urban intellectuals inspired by Fidel Castro and Che Guevara. Began a dialogue with Colombian officials in 1999, following a campaign of mass kidnappings—each involving at least one U.S. citizen—to demonstrate its strength and continuing viability and force the Andres Pastrana administration to negotiate. Peace talks between Bogotá and the ELN, started in 1999, continued sporadically but once again had broken down by year's end. [Contacts between Bogotá and the ELN had resumed by the end of 2003. The ELN also concluded a strategic cooperation agreement with the Revolutionary Armed Forces of Colombia (FARC) in the fall of 2003, and has since formed integrated fighting units.]

Activities
Kidnapping, hijacking, bombing, and extortion. Minimal conventional military capability. Annually conducts hundreds of kidnappings for ransom, often targeting foreign employees of large corporations, especially in the petroleum industry. Derives some revenue from taxation of the illegal narcotics industry. Frequently assaults energy infrastructure and has inflicted major damage on pipelines and the electricity distribution network.

Strength
Approximately 3,000 to 5,000 armed combatants and an unknown number of active supporters.

Location/ Area of Operation
Mostly in rural and mountainous areas of northern, northeastern, and southwestern Colombia and the Venezuela border regions.

External Aid
Cuba provides some medical care and political consultation.

REVOLUTIONARY ARMED FORCES OF COLOMBIA (FUERZAS ARMADAS REVOLUCIONARIOS DE COLOMBIA, OR FARC)—COLOMBIA

Description
Established in 1964 as the military wing of the Colombia Communist Party, the FARC is Colombia's oldest, largest, most capable, and best-equipped Marxist insurgency. The FARC is governed by a secretariat, led by the septuagenarian Manuel Marulanda (a.k.a. "Tirofijo") and six others, including the senior military commander Jorge Briceno (a.k.a. "Jojoy"). Organized along military lines and includes several urban fronts. In February 2002, the group's slow-moving peace negotiation process with the Pastrana administration was terminated by Bogotá following the group's plane hijacking and kidnapping of a Colombian senator from the aircraft. On August 7, 2002, the FARC launched a large-scale mortar attack on the presidential palace where President Alvaro Uribe was being inaugurated. High-level foreign delegations—including from the United States—attending the inauguration were not injured, but twenty-one residents of a poor neighborhood nearby were killed by a stray round in the attack.

Activities
Bombings, murder, mortar attacks, kidnapping, extortion, hijacking, as well as guerilla and conventional military action against Colombian political, military, and economic targets. In March 1999, the FARC executed three U.S. Indian-rights activists on Venezuelan territory after it kidnapped them in Colombia. Foreign citizens are often targets of FARC kidnapping for ransom. The group has

well-documented ties to a full range of narcotics trafficking activities, including taxation, cultivation, and distribution.

Strength
Approximately 9,000 to 12,000 armed combatants and several thousand more supporters, mostly in rural areas.

Location/ Area of Operation
Colombia, with some activities—extortion, kidnapping, logistics, and rest and recuperation—in Venezuela, Panama, and Ecuador.

External Aid
Cuba provides some medical care and political consultation. A trial is currently underway in Bogotá to determine whether three members of the Irish Republican Army—arrested in Colombia in 2001 upon exiting the FARC-controlled demilitarized zone (*despeje*)—provided advanced explosives training to the FARC.

SHINING PATH (SENDERO LUMINOSO, OR SL)—PERU

Description
Former university professor Abimael Guzman formed the SL in Peru in the late 1960s and his teachings created the foundation of SL's military Maoist doctrine. In the 1980s, SL became one of the most ruthless terrorist groups in the Western Hemisphere—approximately 30,000 people have died since it took up arms in the 1980s. The Peruvian government made dramatic gains against SL during the 1990s, but reports of a recent involvement in narcotrafficking indicate that it may have a new source of funding with which to sustain a resurgence. Its stated goal is to destroy existing Peruvian institutions and replace them with a communist peasant revolutionary regime. It also opposes any influence by foreign governments, as well as by other Latin American guerilla troops, especially the Tupac Amaru Revolutionary Movement (MRTA).

In 2002, eight suspected SL members were arrested on suspicion of complicity in the March 20 bombing across the street from the U.S. embassy, which killed ten people. They are being held pending charges, which could take up to one year. Lima has been very aggressive in prosecuting terrorist suspects in 2002. According to the Peruvian National Police Intelligence Directorate, 199 suspected terrorists were arrested between January and mid-November [2002]. Counterterrorist operations targeted pockets of terrorist activity in the Upper Huallaga River Valley and the Apurimac/Ene River Valley, where SL columns continued to conduct periodic attacks.

Activities
Conducted indiscriminate bombing campaigns and selective assassinations. Detonated explosives at diplomatic missions of several countries in Peru in 1990, including an attempt to car bomb the U.S. embassy in December. Peruvian authorities continued operations against the SL in 2002 in the countryside, where the SL conducted periodic raids on villages.

Strength
Membership is unknown but estimated to be 400 to 500 armed militants. SL's strength has been vastly diminished by arrests and desertions but appears to be growing again, possibly due to involvement in narcotrafficking.

Location/Area of Operation
Peru, with most activity in rural areas.

External Aid
None.

UNITED SELF-DEFENSE FORCES/GROUP OF COLOMBIA (AUTODEFENSAS UNIDAS DE COLOMBIA, OR AUC)—COLOMBIA

Description
The AUC—commonly referred to as paramilitaries—is an umbrella organization formed in April 1997 to consolidate most local and regional paramilitary groups, each with the mission to protect economic interests and combat FARC and ELN insurgents locally. During 2002, the AUC leadership dissolved and then subsequently reconstituted most of the organization, claiming to be trying to purge it of the factions most heavily involved in narcotrafficking. The AUC is supported by economic elites, drug traffickers, and local communities lacking effective government support and claims that its primary objective is to protect its sponsors from insurgents. It is adequately equipped and armed and reportedly pays its members a monthly salary.

Activities
AUC operations vary from assassinating suspected insurgent supporters to engaging guerilla combat units. AUC political leader Carlos Castano has claimed that 70 percent of the AUC's operational costs are financed with drugs-related earnings, the rest from "donations" from AUC sponsors.

Since December 2002, the paramilitary groups under Carlos Castano's influence have adopted a ceasefire and are exploring peace negotiations with Bogotá. The AUC generally avoids actions against U.S. personnel or interests.

Strength
Estimated 6,000 to 8,150, including former military and insurgent personnel. [AUC strength was estimated between 13,000 and 19,000 fighters at the end of 2003.]

Location/Area of Operation
AUC forces are strongest in the northwest in Anioquia, Cordoba, Sucre, and Bolivar departments. Since 1999, the group demon-

strated a growing presence in other northern and southwestern departments. Clashes between the AUC and FARC insurgents in Putumayo in 2000 demonstrated the range of the AUC to contest insurgents throughout Colombia.

External Aid
None.

With the exception of bracketed material, all descriptions excerpted from "Appendix B: Background Information on Designated Foreign Terrorist Organizations," Patterns of Global Terrorism, 2002 (U.S. Department of State Coordinator for Counterterrorism, April 2003), available at http://www.state.gov/documents/organization/20177.pdf.

APPENDIX D:
ACRONYMS AND ABBREVIATIONS

ACI – Andean Counterdrug Initiative
AFTA – Andean Free Trade Agreement
ATPA – Andean Trade Preference Act
ATPDEA – Andean Trade Promotion and Drug Eradication Act
AUC – United Self-Defense Forces of Colombia
AWACS – Airborne warning and control system
CAF – Corporación Andina de Fomento (Andean Finance Corporation)
CAFTA – Central American Free Trade Agreement
Caricom – Caribbean Community and Common Market
CAS – Country assistance strategy
CIAT – Inter-American Center of Tax Administrations
CICAD – Inter-American Drug Abuse Control Commission
CIFTA – Inter-American Convention against Illicit Manufacturing of and Trafficking in Firearms, Ammunitions, Explosives, and Other Related Materials
DEA – Drug Enforcement Administration
DNE – Dirección Nacional de Estupefacientes, Colombia
ECLAC – Economic Commission for Latin America and the Caribbean (United Nations)
ELN – National Liberation Army
ESW – Economic and sector work
EU – European Union
FAO – Food and Agriculture Organization (United Nations)
FARC – Revolutionary Armed Forces of Colombia
FTA – Free trade agreement
FTAA – Free Trade Area of the Americas
GDP – Gross domestic product
HAP – Humanitarian Action Plan (United Nations)

IBRD – International Bank for Reconstruction and
   Development (World Bank Group)
ICC – International Criminal Court
ICO – International Coffee Organization
IDA – International Development Association (World Bank
   Group)
IDB – Inter-American Development Bank
IDP – Internally displaced persons
IEEPA – International Emergencies Economic Powers Act
IFI – International financial institution
ILEA – International Law Enforcement Academy
ILO – International Labor Organization
IMF – International Monetary Fund
INL – Bureau of International Narcotics and Law
   Enforcement (U.S. State Department)
ITC – International Trade Commission
MCA – Millennium Challenge Account
MEM – Multilateral Evaluation Mechanism (Organization of
   American States)
Mercosur – Mercado Comun del Sur (Southern Cone Com-
   mon Market)
MFI – Microfinance institution
MPA – Maritime patrol aircraft
NATO – North Atlantic Treaty Organization
NGO – Nongovernmental organization
OAS/OEA – Organization of American States/Organización
   de Estados Americanos
OFAC – Office of Foreign Assets Control (U.S. Treasury
   Department)
ONDCP – Office of National Drug Control Policy
OPIC – Overseas Private Investment Corporation
RSS – Social Solidarity Network (Colombia)
SIVAM – System for the Vigilance of the Amazon
SNAIPD – National System of Integral Assistance to the
   Population Displaced by Violence
South Com – U.S. Southern Command (U.S. Department of
   Defense)

Appendixes

UNHCHR – UN High Commissioner for Human Rights
UNHCR – UN High Commissioner for Refugees
UNODC – UN Office on Drugs and Crime
USAID – U.S. Agency for International Development
USTR – U.S. Trade Representative
VAT – Value-added tax

APPENDIX E:
COMMISSION MEETINGS AND CONSULTATIONS

Note: Because all meetings were conducted according to Council on Foreign Relations rules, the identity of individuals is not listed publicly.

COLOMBIA

Business
ANDI, Colombian Federation of Businesses
BanColombia
COINVERTIR, Invest in Colombia Corporation
Colombian National Chocolate Company
Corfinsura
Gerente Investments
Grupo Corona
SurAmericana

Government
Attorney General
Central Bank Board of Directors
Commander in Chief of the Armed Forces
Constitutional Court Magistrates
Director, National Police
Foreign Minister
High Commissioner for Peace
Ministry of Defense
Ministry of National Planning
Ombudsman
Vice President

International Community, U.S. Embassy, and Foreign Ambassadors
France
Mexico
Norway
Sweden
United Nations Human Rights office in Colombia (UNHCHR)
United Nations Development Programme Mission to Colombia (UNDP)
United Nations High Commissioner for Refugees in Colombia (UNHCR)
United Nations Children's Fund (UNICEF)
U.S. Ambassador
U.S. Embassy staff

Media
El Tiempo
Semana

Parliamentarians
Conservative Party
Liberal Party

NGOs
Consultancy for Human Rights and Displacement (CODHES)
Colombian Commission of Jurists
Foundation Ideas Para la Paz (FIP)
Friedrich Ebert Stiftung (FESCOL)

Civil Society Actors
International Committee of the Red Cross
National Commission of Reconciliation
Professors from Universidad de los Andes, Universidad Nacional de Colombia

ECUADOR

Business
Analytica Securities
Banana Exporters Association
Banco de Guayaquil
Investment Promotion in Ecuador Corporation (CORPEI)
Guayaquil Chamber of Commerce
Grupo Seminario Banana Producers
Quito Chamber of Commerce
Flower Exporters Association

Media
Vistazo

Government
Central Bank
Civic Commission against Corruption
Ministry of Defense
Ministry of External Trade and Commerce
National Security Council
Office of the Foreign Ministry
Office of the Joint Chiefs of Staff of the Armed Forces
PetroEcuador
Supreme Court

U.S. Embassy
U.S. Ambassador
U.S. Embassy staff

Parliamentarians
Social Christian Party
Pachakutik

NGOs
Corporation for Development Studies (CEDES)
Fondo Ecuatoriano Populurum Progresso (FEPP)

Civil Society Analysts
Industrial Workers Union (CEOSL)
Banana Workers Union (FENACLE)
Former Presidents and Former Vice President of Ecuador
Professors from the University of Guayaquil, University of the
    Andes

VENEZUELA

Business
Alfonzo Rivas & CiA
Banco Gente
Banco Mercantil
Banco Provincial
Bermudez y Asociados
Citibank
Coindustria
Corpalmar
Venezuelan business association
Mendoza Group
Sivensa
Venezuelan Investment Promotion Agency (CONAPRI)
Venezuelan Stock Exchange
Venezuelan-American Chamber of Commerce

Civil Society Actors
AKSA Partners Pollsters
Datanalisis Pollster
Former Minister of Interior
Office of the Secretary General of Venezuelan Workers'
    Confederation (CTV)
Professors from Instituto de Estudios Superiores de
    Administración, Andres Bello Catholic University,
    Universidad Central

Government
Ministry of Finance
Ministry of Interior and Justice
Attorney General
Foreign Minister
Vice President
Supreme Court

International Financial Institutions
Corporación Andina de Fomento (CAF)
World Bank, Mission team in Venezuela

International Community, U.S. Embassy, and Foreign Ambassadors
Brazil
Chile
Colombia
Ecuador
Mexico
Peru
Spain
U.S. Ambassador
U.S. Embassy staff
United Nations High Commissioner for Refugees Office in Caracas (UNHCR)
United Kingdom

Media
El Nacional
El Universal
RCN TV
Tal Cual

NGOs
Fe y Alegria (Jesuit)
PROVEA (human rights organization)
VenEconomía

Parliamentarians
Acción Democrática
Christian Democrats (COPEI)
Movimiento al Socialismo (MAS)
Movimiento Quinta Republica (MQR)
Primero Justicia

UNITED STATES: WASHINGTON AND NEW YORK–BASED ANALYSTS

Civil Society Analysts
AFL-CIO International Affairs Department
Georgetown University

Foreign Ambassadors in Washington
Colombia
Ecuador
Peru
Venezuela

Government
National Intelligence Council
National Security Council
U.S. Agency for International Development (USAID)
U.S. Department of State
U.S. Southern Command (South Com)

International Financial Institutions
Institute of International Finance
International Monetary Fund – Western Hemisphere Program
World Bank, Office of the Vice President for Latin America

NGOs
Brookings Institution
Center for Strategic and International Studies
Human Rights Watch

Lutheran World Relief/Afro-Colombian NGO
National Defense University
Washington Office on Latin America
Inter-American Defense Board

CPA MISSION STATEMENT

The Center for Preventive Action (CPA) seeks to help prevent deadly conflicts around the world, find ways to resolve ongoing ones, and expand the body of knowledge on conflict prevention. It does so by bringing together representatives of governments, international organizations, nongovernmental organizations, corporations, and civil society to develop and implement practical and timely strategies for promoting peace in specific conflict situations. The CPA focuses on conflicts in countries or regions that affect U.S. interests, where prevention appears possible and when the resources of the Council on Foreign Relations can make a difference. The CPA does this by:

- *Convening Preventive Action Commissions* composed of Council members, staff, and other experts. The Commissions devise a conflict prevention strategy tailored to the particular conflict.
- *Assembling roundtables of experts* to issue timely, concrete policy recommendations that the U.S. government, the international community, and local actors can take to strengthen the hand of those groups committed to resolving differences peacefully.
- *Engaging the U.S. government and news media* in conflict prevention efforts. CPA staff and commission members meet with administration officials and members of Congress, build networks between American officials and key local and external actors, and raise awareness among journalists of potential flashpoints around the globe.
- *Providing a source of expertise on conflict prevention* to include research, case studies, and lessons learned from past conflicts that policymakers and private citizens can use to prevent or mitigate future deadly conflicts.

CPA ADVISORY COMMITTEE